How To Catch Panfish

MINNETONKA, MINNESOTA

Author Dick Sternberg is an accomplished multi-species angler, and panfish rank high on his list of fishing priorities.

How To Catch Panfish

Printed in 2004.

Mike Vail
Vice President,
Products and Business Development

Tom Carpenter
Director of Book and New Media Development

Dan Kennedy
Book Production Manager

Jenya Prosmitsky
Book Design & Production

Gina Germ
Photo Editor

Michele Teigen
Book Development Coordinator

Janice Cauley
Proofreading

Principle Photography
Bill Lindner Photography (Bill Lindner, Mike Hehner, Tom Heck, Pete Cozad, Jason Lund)

Additional Photography
Jerry Robb, pp. 31(3), 32(2), 33(3), 43(4), 75(4), 77(3), 103, 123(6)
Tom Carpenter/NAOG, pp. 11, 15, 17(4), 20, 21(3), 49, 81, 91, 92, 93(3), 132, 139(3), 140(3), 142, 143
Dan Kennedy/NAOG, pp. 19, 51
Steve McAdams, p. 25
Dick Sternberg, pp. 31, 32, 33, 43(2), 48, 62, 63, 75, 83, 115, 119, 132, 133(3), 139(3)
Don Wirth, pp. 32, 76
Mark Emery, pp. 65
Doug Stamm, pp. 75, 76, 79, 102, 128
Roger Peterson, pp. 76, 103
Richard Grost, p. 103
Soc Clay, p. 109
Bill Vanderford, p. 118
Tom Pagliaroli, p. 120
Tom Evans, p. 121

Illustration
Joe Tomelleri, pp. 27, 29, 63, 65, 67, 101, 117, 119, 121;
David Rottinghaus, pp. 39, 40, 41, 44, 51, 53(2), 92, 109, 129 all, 131 all
Duane Raver, p. 63
Dave Schelitzche, pp. 85, 89(2), 111, 147, 151, 153

2 3 4 5 6 7 8 9 / 08 07 06 05 04

© 1999 North American Fishing Club

ISBN 1-58159-062-8

North American Fishing Club
12301 Whitewater Drive
Minnetonka, MN 55343

CONTENTS

INTRODUCTION

In terms of sheer popularity, there is no fish in North America with a bigger following than those lumped together under the heading of "panfish."

Bluegill. Crappie. White bass. Yellow perch. Shellcrackers. Pumpkinseeds. Rock bass. White perch. Most of us cut our angling teeth on these species, but we also realize that panfishing is not just for kids. Bull bluegills can be just as tough to tempt as 10-pound brown trout. And a 2-pound crappie, on most waters, is as rare as a 10-pound bass ... and just as fun to catch!

Whether you call them bulls or slabs or jumbos, panfish share wide ranges and the propensity to school, sometimes in large numbers. But each species is also unique in its habits, habitat preferences and diet; this makes it a challenge to consistently boat larger fish.

This book, *How to Catch Panfish*, will not only take you through the annual movement of the panfish you love to catch, it will highlight specific strategies for taking panfish throughout the year and under all conditions. Some of these methods will work on the waters you fish, others may not; the key is having them in your angling arsenal.

Congratulations to author Dick Sternberg, Tom Carpenter and the rest of our book staff for producing what may well be the finest volume on panfishing ever written. Enjoy the book and catching more and bigger panfish!

Steve Pennaz

Executive Director
North American Fishing Club

5

PANFISHING EQUIPMENT

*O*wning the right gear is just as important for panfish as for bass, catfish or walleyes.

A light spinning rod from 7 to 8½ feet long is ideal for most types of panfish angling. You could use a much shorter rod, but your casting would suffer and you wouldn't be able to place your bait as accurately.

PANFISH RODS & REELS

In selecting panfish gear the general rule is: Go light. Not only does light tackle enable you to cast tiny panfish lures and baits, it adds greatly to the sport by making even a modest-sized fish feel like a big one.

The vast majority of panfishermen use one or more of the following three types of gear:

Spinning Gear

The modern trend in spinning gear is toward longer rods. In years past, long rods were impractical; because the rod materials of the time were comparatively heavy, long rods were too cumbersome for most types of panfish angling. With the lighter, stronger rod materials now available, however, panfishermen can enjoy the benefits of a long rod without the excess weight.

The number-one benefit of a long rod is that it allows you to drop your bait into tight spots. With a short rod, these spots could be reached only by casting, so your chances of tangling in the cover are much greater.

Another advantage: Long rods give you considerably more leverage for casting light lures and rigs. Whatever rod you choose, it should have a soft tip so it flexes easily from the weight of a light lure. Otherwise, you'll be throwing the lure, not casting it.

Your spinning rod should be paired with a lightweight, wide-spool spinning reel, preferably an open-face model. Closed-face reels increase line friction, shortening casting distance and making it more difficult to cast light baits.

Fly-Fishing Gear

There are times when fly fishing will produce more panfish than any other method. But if you're going to fly fish for panfish, don't make the common mistake of using the same outfit that you would for good-sized trout or bass. A 2- to 5-weight graphite rod will suffice for sunfish, crappies or most any other kind of panfish.

In panfish angling, the fly reel does little more than store the line; so it doesn't pay to spend a lot of money on a fancy model. And because there is no need for a lot of backing, it's not necessary to buy a reel with a large line capacity. A small, lightweight, single-action fly reel will do the job.

Extension/Cane Poles

Some fishermen think that cane poles are used only by those who can't afford more sophisticated gear. But the truth is, cane poles and extension poles (their modern-day fiberglass replacements) serve an important purpose. And if you've ever tried casting your bait into a tiny opening in a bed of cane or bulrushes, you know what that purpose is. Your rig will invariable tangle around the tall stems, so you'll spend most of your time getting unsnagged and probably spook the fish.

With a pole from 10 to 16 feet in length, however, you can keep your boat at a distance and set your bait into the precise spot. When you hook a fish, you don't have to reel it in and risk getting it tangled in the weeds; you simply lift it straight up.

Although many anglers still use cane poles, extension poles are rapidly taking over the market. Not only are they much lighter, they collapse to a length of only about 4 feet, so they are much easier to transport.

You can attach a small reel to your cane pole or extension pole, but most anglers simply tie some line to the pole's tip. The line should be just a little longer than the pole. If you make the line too long, you won't be able to accurately place the bait.

A 2- to 5-weight fly rod from 7½ to 9 feet in length will easily cast the flies normally used for panfish, yet is light enough that a decent-sized panfish will give you a good tussle.

An extension pole not only enables you to place your bait in small openings without tangling, it allows you to lift the fish out of the cover before it can wrap your line around stems or branches.

LINES & KNOTS

The beauty of panfish angling is its simplicity—simple tackle, simple techniques and simple lines and knots. But that doesn't mean lines and knots aren't important. Here are some line-selection recommendations and instructions on tying the knots commonly used by panfishermen.

Lines

Selecting the right line for panfish angling usually involves compromise. You could easily land the biggest panfish with 2-pound line, assuming it was hooked in open water. But that is seldom the case; more often, you'll be extracting the fish from a weedbed or brush pile where they will make short work of line that light. This explains why experienced panfishermen normally use 4- to 6-pound test and may go as heavy as 12 in extra-heavy cover.

Limp monofilament is the near-universal choice of those who use spinning tackle. Stiff mono would restrict the action of most small panfish lures and make casting more difficult. To minimize visibility, the line should be clear or match the color of the water. For night fishing, however, some fishermen prefer fluorescent mono used in conjunction with a black light that makes it glow.

Although selecting a fly line for panfish angling is comparatively easy, you still

Selecting Fly Line

Here are the main considerations in selecting a fly line:

Weight

For best casting performance, the weight of your fly line must match the weight of your rod. Most panfish anglers use 2- to 5-weight outfits. The best weight for you depends more on the size of the fly than the size of the fish; a light line may lack the punch to cast a good-sized streamer or wind-resistant popper.

Taper

The way your fly line is tapered affects casting performance and delicacy. Panfishermen normally use *double-taper* (DT) lines, which are tapered on both ends. They work well for short- to medium-distance casting and, because the end is thin, it alights delicately. When one end of the line wears out, the line can simply be reversed. *Weight-forward*

(WF) lines have a thick, heavy front end. They are a good choice for making long casts and punching into the wind, but they lack delicacy. Level lines (L), are the same diameter over their length. They are the least expensive type of fly line, but their casting performance is inferior.

Buoyancy

The buoyancy of your line must suit the type of fly you're using and depth you want to fish. Floating lines (F) are by far the most popular. Because they are impregnated with air bubbles, they float high on the surface and work especially well with dry flies. But they can also be used for subsurface flies. Sinking lines (S) have lead or tungsten particles in the coating and will get you down as deep as 20 feet, but they are difficult to cast. Floating/Sinking (FS), also called sink-tip lines, have a 5- to 25-foot

Check the label on a fly line box to make sure you're getting the right line. The taper is usually listed first, followed by the weight and the buoyancy. A WF-4-F, for example, is a weight-forward, 4-weight, floating line.

sinking tip section; the rest of the line floats. They are much easier to cast than full-sinking lines, but will not fish as deep.

Line Tapers Commonly Used for Panfish

Double-Taper

Weight-Forward

Level

---

have to know the basic line-selection principles (above). For best casting performance, you need to consider line weight and taper. A tapered leader will also improve your casting. The tippet (end sec-

tion) should be no heavier than 4X (4- to 6-pound test).

Knots

The basic knots shown on the following pages will get

you by for most any kind of panfish angling with both spinning and fly-fishing gear.

Attaching Line to Spool of Reel—Arbor Knot

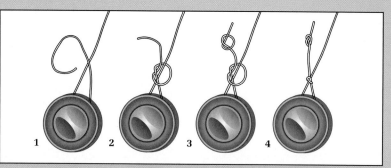

The arbor knot is so named because it tightens firmly around the arbor, preventing the line from slipping when you reel.

(1) Pass the line around the spool; (2) wrap the free end around the standing line and make an overhand knot; (3) make an overhand knot in the free end; (4) snug up the knot by pulling on the standing line; the knot should tighten firmly around the arbor.

Tying on Hook, Lure or Fly—Trilene Knot

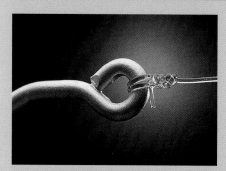

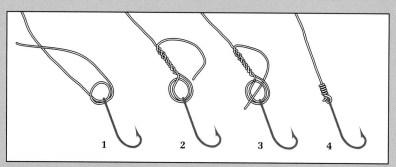

The Trilene knot has a double loop around the hook eye and is one of the strongest hook-attachment knots.

(1) Form a double loop by passing the free end through the hook eye twice; (2) wrap the free end around the standing line 4-5 times; (3) pass the free end through the double loop; (4) pull on the standing line and hook to snug up the knot.

Attaching a Lure to Swing Freely—Loop Knot

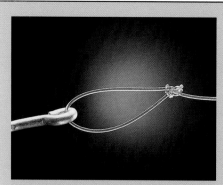

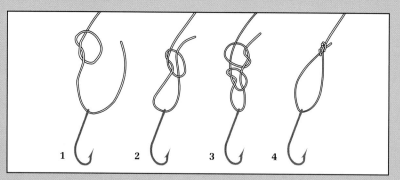

A loop knot allows your lure to swing more freely, so it has better action than a lure that is snubbed down tightly.

(1) Make an overhand knot near the end of the line and put the free end through the lure eye; (2) pass the free end through the overhand knot; (3) with the free end, make an overhand knot around the standing line (where you tie the second overhand determines the size of the loop); (4) tighten the overhand knots and pull the standing line to snug up the knot.

Tying a Bobber Stop—Sliding Stop

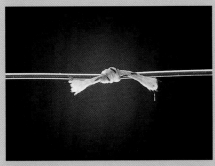

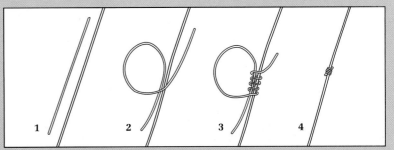

A sliding stop comes in handy for slip-bobber fishing and also has other uses, like marking your depth.

(1) Lay a foot-long piece of Nylon or Dacron line alongside your fishing line, *(2)* form a loop in the short line, as shown, *(3)* pass the free end of the short line through the loop and around the standing line 4-5 times, *(4)* pull on both ends of the short line to snug up the knot. Trim the ends. Slide the knot up and down your fishing line as necessary.

Splicing Monofilament Line or Sections of Fly Leader—Blood Knot

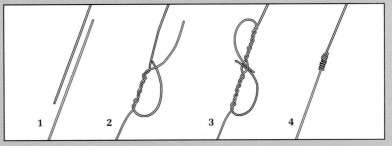

A blood knot looks complex, but is quite simple to tie. Don't try it with lines of greatly different diameters or different materials.

(1) Hold the lines alongside each other, with the ends facing opposite directions; *(2)* wrap one line around the other 4-5 times, and pass the free end between the two lines, as shown; *(3)* repeat step 2 with the other line; *(4)* pull on both lines to snug up the knot. Trim the ends.

Attaching Leader to Fly Line—Tube Knot

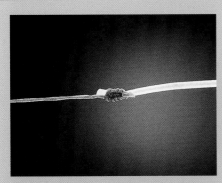

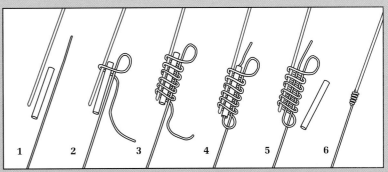

A tube knot is much easier to tie than the nail knot used by many anglers, because you can thread the end of the leader through the tube, rather than the smaller opening made by a nail.

(1) Lay a small plastic drinking straw alongside the end of the fly line; *(2)* wrap the leader butt around the fly line, straw and standing portion of the leader; *(3)* make about 5 wraps, winding toward the end of the fly line; *(4)* push the butt of the leader back through the straw; *(5)* carefully remove the straw; *(6)* pull on both ends of the leader to snug up the knot. Trim.

TERMINAL TACKLE

You can easily carry all of the terminal tackle normally used for panfishing in a small box that fits into your shirt pocket. Here we will discuss the basic items that you need. Specialty items will be covered later when we discuss specific fishing techniques.

Hooks

Most serious panfishermen carry a selection of hooks in sizes 2 to 8, but you may want hooks as large as 1/0 for jumbo crappies or as small as 10 for sunfish.

Light-wire hooks work best for most types of panfishing. They're thin enough that they won't badly damage delicate baits and, should you get snagged, they'll usually bend enough that you can pull free.

Many panfish anglers prefer extra-long-shank hooks because they're much easier to remove when a panfish swallows the bait, and their shank will bend more easily when you get snagged. But short-shank hooks are lighter and less conspicuous, so it's a good idea to carry some of each.

Sinkers

Panfish anglers rely almost exclusively on split-shot for weighting lures and live-bait rigs. With a dispenser containing a variety of split-shot sizes, you'll be ready for most any panfishing situation. If

you'll be fishing in "slop," select the type without "ears" that tend to collect moss.

Floats

There are dozens of different styles of floats used in panfishing, but they fall into two basic categories:
• Fixed floats, such as clip-on or peg-on models, attach securely to the line. They are easy to rig and work well for fishing in shallow water. But if you're fishing deeper than 5 feet, you may have trouble casting because there is too much line dangling from the end of your rod.
• Slip-floats are the best choice for fishing in deep water. A movable knot, called a "sliding stop" (p. 13), can be positioned anywhere along your line to determine your fishing depth.

One of the most common mistakes in panfishing is using a float that is too large. When a fish takes your bait and feels too much resistance, it will probably let go and you may not even notice the bite.

Although most floats are quite inexpensive, some manufacturers are now offering super-sensitive "European-style" floats selling for many times the price of an ordinary float. Most veteran panfishermen still use the more conventional models, but they take great pains to precisely balance them with split-shot so they will telegraph even the lightest bite and offer minimal resistance when a fish pulls them under.

Swivels & Clips

For the majority of pan-fishing, you can get by with no swivels, snaps or clips of any kind, but there are times when they come in handy.

When you're fishing with artificials and changing lures frequently, for example, a small clip greatly speeds up the process. When you're using spoons, spinners or other lures that could twist your line, attach them with a small snap-swivel or splice a small barrel swivel into your line about 18 inches above the lure.

Selecting the Right Panfish Hook

Use a thin-wire hook when fishing with minnows, leeches or other swimming baits. The nearly weightless hooks allow the bait to swim more naturally.

An extra-long-shank hook comes in handy when fishing for sunfish. They tend to swallow the bait and their mouths are so small that you can't get your fingers inside to remove the hook.

Popular Types of Panfish Floats

Slip-Floats. *(1) Pear-shaped Styrofoam tube float; (2) weighted Styrofoam tube float, which requires less weight for balance; (3) wooden tube float, which is more durable than the Styrofoam type; (4) removable slip-float, which can be put on or taken off your line without rerigging; (5) lighted slip-float, for night fishing; (6) casting bubble, which can be partially filled with water for extra casting weight or completely filled for subsurface presentations. It can be affixed to the line or rigged to slip.*

Fixed Floats. *(7) Peg-on styrofoam float, which has a thin shape for good sensitivity; (8) pear-shaped clip-on float, which is more sensitive than an ordinary round float; (9) European-style "high-top" float, which offers maximum sensitivity; (10) spring-lock float.*

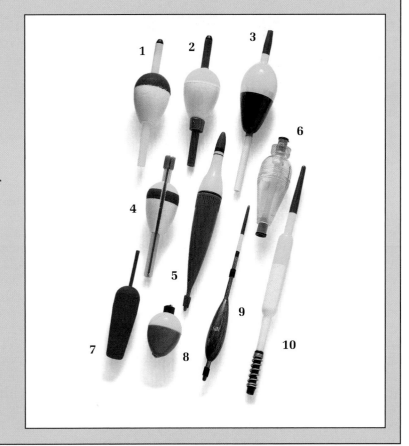

A well-rigged jon boat makes a good all-around panfishing rig.

BOATS, MOTORS & ACCESSORIES

You don't need any particular kind of boat to catch panfish. In fact, a tremendous number of panfish are taken by bank or dock fishermen who don't even own a boat.

Because the majority of panfishing is done on relatively small lakes, river backwaters or protected bays of larger lakes, there is usually no need for a large, deep-hulled boat. But that's not the case if you must cross a large expanse of water to reach your fishing spot or if you're fishing open-water species such as white bass.

If you happen to own a bass boat, you already have the ideal panfish boat. You can use it to get into the shallow, weedy areas where panfish are often found and, once you get there, you can fish in comfort.

A jon boat, though not nearly as plush, serves the same purpose. It draws only a few inches of water and is surprisingly stable for its weight. Most panfishermen opt for 14- to 16-footers rigged with 10- to 25-hp outboards.

Another popular choice is a 14- to 16-foot aluminum semi-V, also rigged with a 10- to 25-hp outboard. A semi-V draws more water than a jon boat, but you won't take as much spray when the water is choppy.

On small lakes and ponds where it would be impossible to launch a regular boat, many anglers opt for float tubes (p. 95) or small inflatable boats.

Because anchoring is important in many types of panfishing, it pays to have some type of anchor-retrieval system, either manual (shown) or electric. Not only will it make anchoring easy, it keeps loose anchor rope out of your way.

A bow-mount trolling motor enables you to move silently through shallow water as you search for panfish. For a 16-foot jon boat or semi-V, you'll need a motor with at least 36 pounds of thrust.

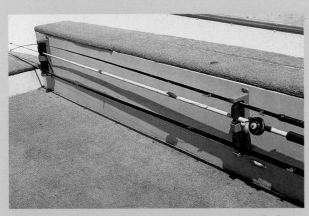

The long rods used in panfishing can easily be broken if they're strewn about the boat. When they're not in use, store them in rod holders secured to the side of the boat.

Carry a duck-billed push pole for making your way through dense weedbeds or very shallow water. The duck bill (inset) spreads when you push it into the mud, giving you something solid to push against.

A brush clamp allows you to tie off to trees, brush or emergent weeds. You won't have to anchor and risk spooking the fish, and you can move from spot to spot more easily.

If you don't have a live well (left), put your panfish in a wire-mesh basket (right) to keep them fresh. This way, the fish can safely be released should you decide you don't want them.

ELECTRONICS

There will be times when you don't need electronics to catch panfish, and there will be times when good electronics are indispensible.

You probably don't need much in the way of electronics when you're sight-fishing for spawning crappies in a shallow bulrush bed. But when you're trying to locate crappies suspended in open water, fishing without a good depth finder would be a waste of time. Most panfishermen prefer liquid-crystal graphs for open-water fishing, although many stick with the same flasher units they use for ice fishing (p. 138).

By the same token, you don't need a GPS unit to find sunfish in the back end of a creek arm. If you found a nice school on a weedy hump in the middle of the lake, however, and you want to go back to the spot, a GPS unit will save you a lot of exploring.

Underwater video cameras are also finding a niche in panfishing. When you spot a school of fish on your depth finder but you're not really sure what they are, you can drop the camera down and find out.

On the opposite page are the most popular types of electronics used by panfishermen and some tips on using them.

Good electronics are a must for finding suspended panfish in open water.

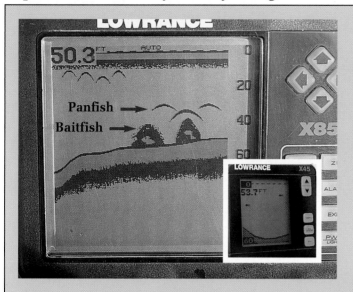

A liquid-crystal graph with at least 160 vertical pixels is sensitive enough that you can distinguish between panfish and schools of baitfish. Some liquid crystals have an optional display that shows fish symbols (inset) instead of true fish marks. Keep your graph set to show the true marks; otherwise, a clump of insect larvae, a few minnows, a leaf or any other object in the water will appear to be a fish.

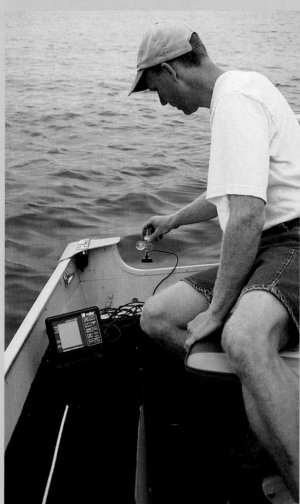

When using a rental boat or one borrowed from a friend, use a portable, battery-operated depthfinder with a transducer that attaches to your transom via suction cups.

Carry a handheld GPS unit so you can punch in the location of hard-to-find spots and return to them later. Keep the unit in a bracket on your boat seat.

Commonly used bait containers include (1) styrofoam crawler box; (2) thick styrofoam bucket for minnows and leeches; (3) snuff box filled with sawdust for waxworms and other grubs; (4) flow-through minnow bucket; (5) cricket/grasshopper dispenser.

ODDS & ENDS

Although panfish anglers generally travel light, there are a few pieces of equipment that can make life much easier—and maybe even put a few more fish in your boat.

You probably won't need all the gear shown on these pages but, depending on what type of panfishing you'll be doing, you'll undoubtedly need some of it.

Besides the equipment featured here, you'll find other gear intended for specific fishing purposes throughout the remainder of the book.

Why You Need Polarized Sunglasses

Polarized sunglasses not only help protect your eyes, they remove glare from the water so you can see panfish in shallow water. The photo at left is an unpolarized view of a colony of spawning beds. The photo at right shows the same beds seen through polarized sunglasses.

In warm weather, carry your bait containers in a large cooler. A couple of 1-liter pop bottles full of ice will keep the bait cool and healthy all day.

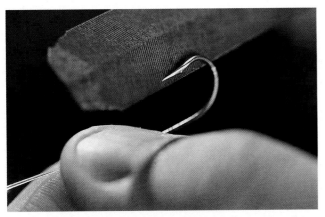

Use a hook file or hone to touch up the point of a new hook or resharpen one that you've been using for awhile. An extra-sharp hook will greatly improve your hooking percentage.

Use marker buoys to pinpoint spawning beds in the shallows or schools of fish on midlake structure.

Carry a nail clipper on a lanyard for cutting lines, trimming knots, etc. With a lanyard, the clipper will always be close at hand.

Remove deeply embedded hooks with a hemostat, a long-handled tool that will fit inside the small mouth of a panfish.

CRAPPIES

*M*ost anglers think of crappie fishing as a springtime-only sport, but we'll show you methods that will help you catch these speckled scrappers all year.

CRAPPIE BASICS

The recent explosion of interest in crappie fishing is testament to the widespread appeal of these mysterious gamefish. As every veteran crappie angler knows, catching "slab" crappies consistently is every bit as difficult as catching big bass, walleyes or trout.

It's not that big crappies are all that scarce. They can be found in numerous lakes, reservoirs and rivers across the country. Anglers have good luck catching them in spring, when they're in the vicinity of their spawning areas, but then the fish just seem to disappear. A few astute fishermen are able to hunt them down in open water during the summer months, but most anglers don't even bother—they say the fish quit biting and there is no use.

Crappies belong to the sunfish family (*Centrarchidae*) and, like all other members of the family, are considered warmwater fish. All centrarchids are nest builders; the male sweeps out a depression with his tail, fertilizes the eggs, guards them until they hatch and continues to guard the fry until they leave the nest.

But crappies differ from other members of the sunfish family in one very important way: They are much more tolerant of low levels of dissolved oxygen, so they are better able to survive during severe winters when a thick blanket of snow covers the ice, preventing sunlight from penetrating to the vegetation and producing oxygen through photosynthesis.

This unique trait explains why crappies are found in practically every kind of warmwater environment— even in shallow, muddy lakes that hold no fish other than crappies, bullheads and maybe a few other kinds of roughfish.

Adding to the mystery surrounding crappies is the cyclical nature of their populations. In many waters, crappies get off a huge hatch about once every 3 to 5 years. These small fish then compete heavily for food, so their growth is stunted. For the next few years, anglers catch only small crappies.

Eventually, fishing pressure and natural mortality take their toll and the remaining fish start to grow rapidly. Anglers haul in limits of slabs for the next year or two, then the cycle repeats itself.

For consistent crappie-fishing success, you must plan your fishing to coincide with natural crappie cycles and shed the idea that crappies can be caught only during the spring. In this chapter, we'll show you how to catch crappies in practically any situation you're likely to encounter.

The burgeoning interest in crappie fishing is evidenced by the increasing popularity of crappie tournaments. Crappie anglers from all over the country now gather to participate in national events.

BLACK CRAPPIE

(Pomoxis nigromaculatus)

The black crappie, as its name suggests, has a somewhat darker coloration than its cousin, the white crappie, but the difference is not always distinct. Coloration varies considerably in different waters and at different times of the year. During the spawning period, for example, males of both species have an overall blackish look.

Black crappies thrive in clear, weedy natural and man-made lakes and are also found in backwaters and slow-moving reaches of warmwater rivers and streams. They prefer clearer, deeper, cooler water than white crappies, favoring water temperatures in the low 70s.

In spring, when water temperatures rise into the low 60s, male black crappies begin making nests, usually

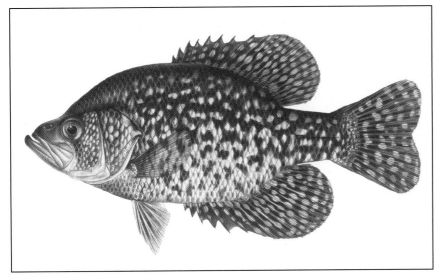

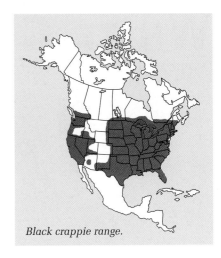

Black crappie range.

Black crappies have 7 or 8 spines on the dorsal fin and are deeper-bodied than whites. At spawning time, males turn much darker than females. Black speckles on the silvery green sides explain why crappies (black and white) are often called specks, speckled perch or calico bass.

World Record: 6 pounds; Westwego Canal, Louisiana; November 28, 1969.

in brushy cover or in stands of emergent vegetation remaining from the previous year. The fish often spawn in colonies, with many individual nests in close proximity. After spawning has been completed, the male guards the nest until the fry disperse.

Adult black crappies feed primarily on small fish, but they also eat immature aquatic insects and large quantities of zooplankton. Their plankton-eating habits explain why they spend so much of their time suspended in open water.

In clearwater lakes, black crappies do most of their feeding around dusk or dawn, or after dark. But in dingy water, they may feed at any time of the day. They continue to feed through the winter months and are a favorite target of ice fishermen.

Black crappies tend to grow slightly faster in the southern part of their range than in the northern part, but no matter where they're found, their growth rate is highly variable, depending mainly on food availability and fishing pressure.

Although black crappies may live up to 10 years, their normal life span is only half that long. It generally takes about 7 years for a black crappie to reach 1 pound.

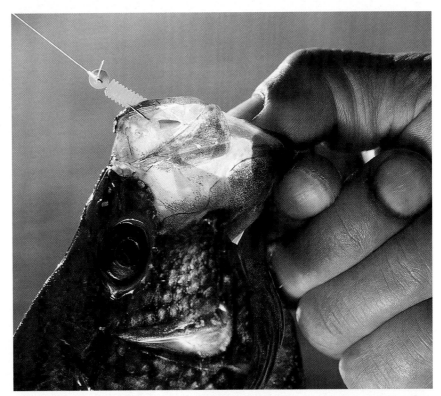

The paper-thin membrane around a crappie's mouth accounts for the name "papermouth." If you try to horse a crappie in or hoist it out of the water, the membrane may rip.

WHITE CRAPPIE

(Pomoxis annularis)

The white crappie's shad-eating habits explain its rapid growth in many southern waters.

In reservoirs of the central United States, white crappies far outnumber blacks, comprising more than 90 percent of the total crappie population.

Besides reservoirs, white crappies inhabit natural lakes and slow-moving portions of rivers and streams—the same types of waters inhabited by blacks. In fact, it's not uncommon for anglers to catch both kinds on the same outing. Although both species can be found in exactly the same habitat, white crappies are more tolerant of warmer, dingier water. They prefer water temperatures from the low to mid 70s and can withstand temperatures up to 85°F. Strangely, white crappies are not found in Florida.

Another important difference: White crappies are less tolerant of brackish water, so they are far less common in brackish rivers along the Atlantic and Gulf coasts.

White and black crappies have similar feeding habits. They eat the same types of foods, with small fish being their favorite. In reservoirs of the southern and central U.S., for example, shad are the predominant food item. When the opportunity presents itself, white crappies also graze on suspended zooplankton in open water.

Although whites tend to feed most heavily around dusk and dawn, they're commonly caught in midday, especially in low-clarity waters. Night fishing is the best option on very clear lakes.

White crappies are spring spawners. When the water temperature reaches the low 60s, males begin sweeping out nests on a firm to slightly soft bottom. They commonly nest under tree roots or overhanging vegetation along a bank. If the water is dingy, nests are usually in 3 feet of water or less; if it's clear, 10 feet or more. Like black crappies, whites usually nest in tight colonies. Once spawning has been completed, males guard the nests until the young swim away.

White crappies usually grow faster than blacks, particularly in southern waters. There, a white crappie could easily reach a weight of 1 pound in

White Crappie

Black Crappie

Compared to black crappies, whites have a more silvery appearance, explaining why they're sometimes called silver bass. Like black crappies, they're also called specks, speckled perch, calico bass and many other regional names.

4 years; it may take a black twice that long to reach the same size. But white crappies

have a shorter life span than blacks, rarely reaching an age of more than 7.

White crappies, like blacks, have silvery green sides with dark specks, but the specks are usually arranged in 7 to 9 vertical bars. White crappies have 5 or 6 spines on the dorsal fin, and the forehead has a deeper depression than that of the black crappie. At spawning time, male white crappies become much darker than females.

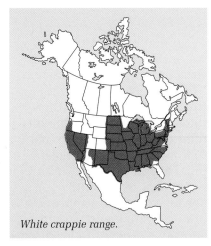

White crappie range.

World Record: 5 pounds, 3 ounces; Enid Dam, Mississippi; July 31, 1957.

WHERE TO FIND CRAPPIES

No matter what type of water crappies live in, their seasonal movements are controlled by the same forces. But how they react to those forces varies, depending on the habitat available to them.

In early spring, for example, crappies are drawn to the water that warms first because that warming water draws baitfish and provides an easy source of food. In natural lakes, crappies often move into shallow, mud-bottomed bays, because the dark-colored bottom absorbs sunlight and heats up rapidly. Most reservoirs, however, do

not have bays of this type, so the fish move into the back ends of creek arms, often where there is an inlet stream to carry in warmer water.

But the areas that draw fish in spring are not necessarily well suited for spawning. If crappies were to spawn in a mud-bottomed bay, for instance, the soft mud would suffocate the eggs. Consequently, the fish seek out spawning areas with a firm bottom and some type of weedy or woody cover to protect the fry. In natural lakes, crappies can find the proper spawning habitat in beds of

bulrushes, maidencane or other emergent weeds that grow on a firm, sandy bottom. In reservoirs, sand-gravel points with brushy cover are a good option.

In summer and early fall, the main priorities for crappies are finding food and comfortable water temperatures. In natural lakes, they often relate to weedbeds, because that's where most kinds of baitfish hang out. But in reservoirs, they may roam open water in pursuit of shad.

As winter approaches and the water cools, the metabolism of crappies slows considerably. They usually move to deeper water where the temperature is a few degrees warmer. In natural lakes, they often congregate in the deepest holes; in reservoirs, in deep areas of the old river channel.

The pages that follow will give you some ideas on where to find crappies in various types of waters. You may find, however, that specific seasonal locations are somewhat different on the waters you fish.

Crappie Location in Natural Lakes During...

Early Spring
- Shallow mud-bottom bays.
- Dead-end channels.
- Harbors and marinas.
- Channels between lakes.

Shallow mud-bottom bay.

Dead-end channel.

Summer and Early Fall
- On deep rock piles.
- On weedy humps.
- Along irregular weedlines.
- On gradually tapering points.

Late Fall and Winter
- Along inside turns on deep weedlines.
- In deep holes.
- On deep flats.
- Off the edge of steep points.

Bulrush point.

- Off the edge of deep sunken islands and rock piles.

Channel between two lakes.

Spring (spawning)
- Sheltered bays and shorelines with a firm bottom and emergent weeds.
- Dead-end channels.
- Shallow points and humps with emergent weeds.
- Beneath overhanging tree limbs or vegetation along a bank.

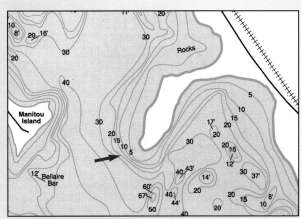

Edge of steep point.

Crappie Location in Man-Made Lakes During...

Early Spring
- Points at mouths of creek arms (pre-spawn staging areas).
- Along edges of creek channels.
- Secondary creek arms.
- Marinas.
- Shallow coves on main lake.
- Mouths of flowing creeks.

Spring (spawning)
- Brushy back ends of creek arms.

- Feeder creeks with woody cover.
- Gravelly points in creek arms.
- Shallow coves on main lake.
- Stump fields in protected coves.

Summer and Early Fall
- Edges of main river channel.
- Edges of creek channels.
- Channel intersections.
- Main-lake points.

- Suspended in flooded timber.
- "Stake Beds" and other man-made fish attractors.

Late Fall and Winter
- Main river channel.
- Deep creek channels.
- Sharp shoreline breaks.
- Off deep main-lake points.
- Deep main-lake coves.

Mouth of flowing creek.

Gravelly point in creek arm.

Edge of creek channel.

Brushy back end of creek arm.

Main-lake point.

Crappie Location in Rivers During...

Early Spring through Spawning
- Shallow, dead-end sloughs and other backwaters off the main river.
- Shallow sandbars.
- Stump fields in backwaters.

Late Spring to Early Fall
- Sloughs with current.
- Deep holes in backwaters.
- Side channels leading into backwaters.
- Deep eddies.
- Deep outside bends.
- Undercut banks and ledges.

Late Fall and Winter
- Deep holes in backwaters or connected "oxbows."
- Deep outside bends in main channel.
- Deep eddies in main channel.

Stumps and standing timber in a backwater.

Slough with current.

Side channel leading to backwater.

Dead-end slough off river.

CRAPPIE-FISHING BASICS

Most experienced crappie anglers will tell you that their biggest challenge is locating the fish. But presentation is important as well. Here are some things to keep in mind when planning your crappie-fishing strategy:

• **Quiet and subtle.** Compared to most other kinds of panfish, crappies are extraordinarily skittish. Scuba divers have no trouble swimming right up to schools of sunfish, but when they try to approach crappies, the fish slip away.

This edginess has obvious implications for anglers: Don't put your boat right on top of the fish, keep noise and movement to a minimum and use a subtle presentation to minimize spooking.

• **Weather/Time of Day.** The daily movements of crappies reflect their strong sensitivity to light. As a rule, they move shallower, stray farther from cover and feed more heavily under dim-light conditions, especially in clear water. This explains why fishing tends to be best in cloudy weather, early or late in the day or at night.

In dingy waters, however, crappies usually bite better on sunny days and the action is faster in midday than in morning and evening. Seldom is there any "night bite."

The wind is also an important consideration. Not only does wave action reduce light penetration, the wind tends to pile up plankton along downwind shorelines, and crappies move in to feed on zooplankton or the baitfish that it attracts.

• **Stay mobile.** Crappies are

Use a landing net for boating a slab crappie. If you attempt to hoist it in, the hook may tear out of its delicate mouth.

the "gypsies" of freshwater gamefish. They go where the food is and you must be willing and able to move along with them.

Instead of staying put and waiting for the fish to start biting, successful crappie anglers spend a lot of time scouting with their electronics. They not only look for crappies around likely cover or structure, they try to spot fish suspended over open water.

• **Fish "high."** Crappies are more likely to swim up for a bait than to go down for one. One glance at a crappie's eye placement should explain why: Its eyes are very close to the top of its head, so it can see upward more easily than downward.

This means you should fish a little shallower than the depth at which you're marking most of the fish. If the

bulk of the school is at 18 to 20 feet, for example, try fishing at 16 or 17.

• **Fish slow.** You may want to use a small spinnerbait, crankbait or other "locator" lure to find crappies but, in most cases, it's a good idea to slow down once you know where they are. Switch to a tiny jig, a minnow beneath a float or some other bait that can be inched along or hung in the fish's face.

• **Not too light.** The standard wisdom in crappie fishing is to use very light tackle. But many fishermen make the mistake of using a whippy rod that makes setting the hook almost impossible. And some spool up with line so light that they risk breaking off any good-sized fish they hook. Light (but not ultra-light) spinning tackle with 4- to 6-pound mono is ideal for most types of crappie fishing.

Crappie Baits

Because of the crappie's fish-eating habits, minnows are far and away the most popular type of live bait. And of all the common types of minnows, fatheads are far and away the number-one choice of crappie anglers. In fact, most bait shops label small fatheads as "crappie minnows." In some areas, however, they're called "tuffies" or "mudminnows."

Fatheads in the 1½- to 2-inch range are recommended for most crappie fishing but, for slab crappies, some anglers prefer 3-inchers.

There are several reasons for the popularity of fatheads: They are widely available, tough enough to stand repeated casting and easy to keep alive.

When the water is cool (below 60°F), however, some veteran crappie fishermen swear by shiners. Not only are they the natural forage in many crappie waters, they produce more flash than fatheads. But when the water warms up, they are difficult to keep alive.

Small dace also make good crappie bait; they are hardier than shiners but not as tough as fatheads. Bait shops may carry several different species, with redbelly dace (also called "rainbows") being the most common.

Crappies will take many other kinds of live bait and there will be times when some of these offerings work even better than minnows. Larval baits, such as waxworms, Eurolarvae and even mayfly wigglers are gaining in popularity for both open-water and ice fishing, and some southern anglers contend that nothing will catch crappies like grass shrimp. It's not unusual for sunfishermen to catch crappies while using small leeches, pieces of nightcrawler, garden worms, crickets, grasshoppers and other baits more commonly considered sunfish fare.

Keep shiners and other sensitive baitfish alive longer in warm weather by adding stress-reducing chemicals to the water.

Popular Crappie Baits

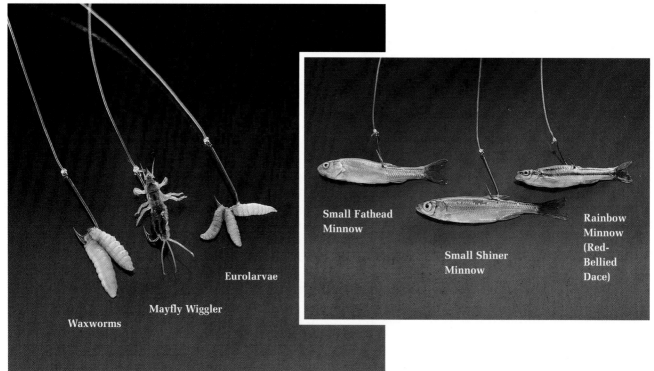

Waxworms

Mayfly Wiggler

Eurolarvae

Small Fathead Minnow

Small Shiner Minnow

Rainbow Minnow (Red-Bellied Dace)

Crappie Lures

Although artificial lures account for considerably fewer crappies than live bait, one type of artificial can be found in the tackle box of practically every crappie angler: the leadhead jig.

The main reason jigs are so effective is that they resemble minnows, the crappie's favorite food. Ordinary round-head jigs are most popular, although many anglers prefer slow-sinking "slider" heads or jigs with some kind of spinner or propeller to slow the sink rate and provide more flash. The majority of crappie jigs have soft-plastic or marabou dressings, although tinsel, bucktail, squirrel tail and hackle dressings are also popular. Most crappie anglers use small jigs ranging in weight from ¹⁄₆₄ to ¹⁄₈ ounce.

You can fish a jig plain or tip it with a small minnow or some other type of live bait. Tipping is usually not necessary in dingy water but may be a big help in very clear water.

Other widely used artificials include spinnerbaits, in-line spinners, minnowbaits, crankbaits, bladebaits and jigging spoons, all in small sizes.

Fly fishing for crappies is not as popular as fly fishing for sunfish. Crappies are far less inclined to feed on the surface, so they seldom take fly-rod bugs or poppers. They will, however, take a variety of minnow-imitating wet flies and small streamers (p. 57).

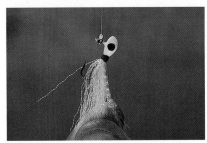

Always tie a jig directly to your line so the knot is in the middle of the attachment eye (top); this way it will hang horizontally and look like a minnow. If the jig hangs vertically (bottom) it will look unnatural.

Popular Crappie Lures

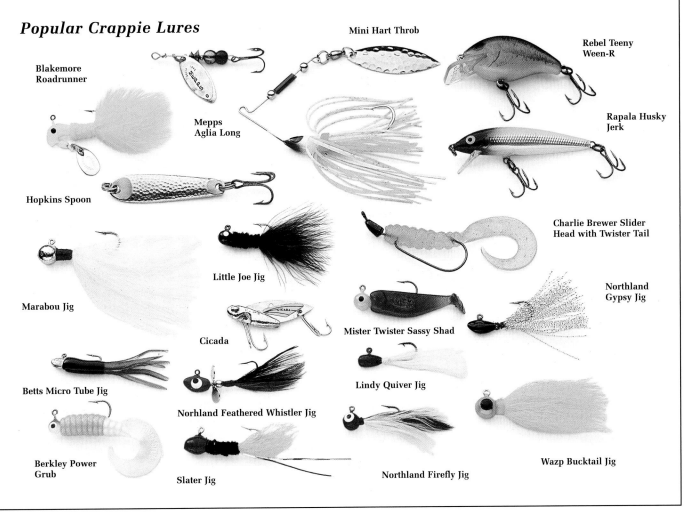

Mini Hart Throb

Rebel Teeny Ween-R

Blakemore Roadrunner

Mepps Aglia Long

Rapala Husky Jerk

Hopkins Spoon

Charlie Brewer Slider Head with Twister Tail

Little Joe Jig

Northland Gypsy Jig

Marabou Jig

Mister Twister Sassy Shad

Cicada

Lindy Quiver Jig

Betts Micro Tube Jig

Norhland Feathered Whistler Jig

Berkley Power Grub

Slater Jig

Northland Firefly Jig

Wazp Bucktail Jig

Crappies prefer broad-leaved weeds, like cabbage, because they provide plenty of shade.

FISHING IN SUBMERGED WEEDS

Crappies are not as weed-oriented as sunfish, but they commonly relate to various kinds of weedy cover, mainly submergent and emergent varieties. Seldom will you find them beneath a dense blanket of lily pads or other floating-leaf vegetation.

How closely crappies relate to the weeds depends mainly on water clarity. The clearer the water, the tighter they hold to the vegetation. In very murky water, weeds are usually absent in water more than a few feet deep so they have little to do with crappie location.

As a rule, crappies will choose broad-leaved vegetation, such as cabbage (above), over stringy or narrow-leaf types. And they prefer sparse weeds that allow them to move about and feed, versus dense, closely spaced vegetation that restricts their movement.

Although there will be times when you'll find crappies right in the weeds, more often they'll be suspended over the weed tops, holding between weed clumps on a broad flat or at key locations along along the weedline (below), which is the deep edge of the submerged vegetation.

How you go about catching crappies in weedy cover depends mainly on what type of weeds they're using. The most productive methods for fishing crappies in submerged weeds are described on the following pages.

Techniques for catching crappies in emergent vegetation will be covered in the section on fishing for crappies at spawning time (p. 46).

Fishing Crappies along a Weedline

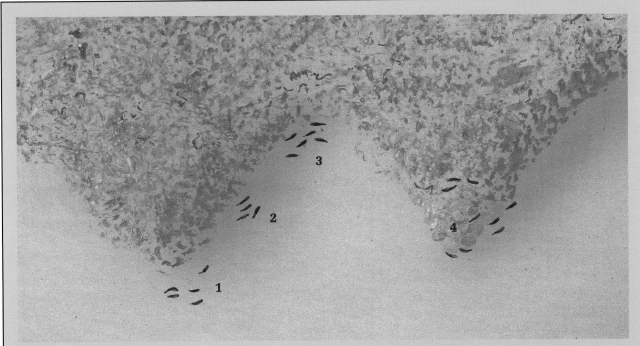

Crappies are not uniformly distributed along a weedline. They tend to concentrate around features such as (1) points, (2) shady areas, (3) inside turns and (4) rocky or gravelly areas. They are not likely to hold along a straight, uniform weed edge, especially where the bottom is soft. In midday, sunlight often pushes the fish away from the weedline and into deeper water where they may suspend.

Locate crappies along a weedline by slow-trolling with a jig. Use your electric trolling motor to closely follow the weed edge. For precise boat control, troll forward if you're using a bow mount and backtroll with a transom mount.

When you catch a crappie, toss out a marker and then work the spot thoroughly by casting with a jig or slip-bobbering with a minnow. Be sure to make a few casts toward open water to catch any crappies that are suspended off the weedline.

Fishing Crappies on a Weed Flat

Density of vegetation on a typical weed flat decreases as the water gets deeper. On the inshore portion of this weed flat, the vegetation is too dense to hold crappies, with the exception of (1) a deep hole and (2) a rock pile. But as the water gets deeper, the weeds thin out. You'll find crappies scattered among (3) loosely spaced weeds or (4) between weed clumps at the outer edge of the flat.

Fancast with a small spinnerbait to locate crappies scattered on a weed flat. A spinnerbait enables you to cover a lot of water in a hurry and its safety-pin shaft (left) is relatively weedless. When the lure reaches an opening in the weeds, stop reeling, let it helicopter into the pocket (right) and then continue your retrieve. When you find some crappies, switch to a slower, more thorough presentation.

Fishing Crappies Over Weed Tops

Make a slip-bobber rig by tying a slip-bobber knot (p. 13) on your line and then adding a small bead, the bobber, a size 4 to 6 hook and enough split shot to balance the rig.

Set the bobber to keep your bait just above the weed tops. Then cast the rig upwind and allow it to drift over the weeds. Vary the placement of each cast to make parallel drifts a few feet apart (see p. 84 for diagram).

Tips for Fishing Submerged Vegetation

When fishing crappies on a weedy hump, pay attention to the angle of the sun; chances are, the fish on (1) the shady side will be more active. Under dim-light conditions, you may find crappies (2) suspended between the weed tops and the surface. When the sun is directly overhead, the fish will either move (3) into the outer fringe of the weeds or (4) away from the hump and suspend in deeper water.

Work a small curlytail jig ($\frac{1}{16}$ to $\frac{1}{32}$ ounce) through submerged weeds. When the open hook catches on the vegetation, give the lure a sharp pop to free it. The erratic action draws the attention of crappies and they strike the jig as it is sinking.

Tie on a slider-head jig for working the weed tops. The flattened head slows the sink rate, so you can work the jig slowly yet control the depth to keep it just brushing the weed tops.

FISHING IN WOODY COVER

Rivers and reservoirs provide some of the country's best crappie fishing—if you know how to extract the fish from the tangle of woody cover.

In the majority of rivers and reservoirs, weed growth is relatively sparse because fluctuating water levels prevent most aquatic plants from taking root. But woody cover is everywhere you look.

Many reservoirs not only have vast expanses of timber that was left standing when the lake was filled, they have hundreds of miles of shoreline that grows up to brush when the water is low and is then flooded when the water level rises. Treetops that have rotted off and fallen into the water, as well as the remaining stumps, also make excellent crappie cover.

In rivers, the current relentlessly erodes the banks, continually toppling trees into the water and washing out roots. Trees and brush carried downstream by floodwaters create massive logjams that may stay put for years.

Although fishing in woody cover can be a challenge, crappies find it irresistible. Not only does it offer shade and overhead protection, it generally holds a plentiful supply of baitfish that are drawn by the invertebrate life clinging to the branches. And in spring, crappies rely on woody cover for spawning habitat.

You can use a variety of methods for fishing in woody cover, but certain rules apply no matter what technique you prefer:
• **Fish vertically.** The more vertical you keep your line, the less chance you will snag in woody cover. Many experienced crappie anglers use a technique called tightlining (p. 44), attaching a heavy sinker to lower their bait into the woody tangle.
• **Use heavy tackle.** Woody cover is not the setting for light tackle. You'll probably want to use mono of at least 8-pound test, and some anglers use 12-pound. To handle line that heavy, you'll need a medium-power spinning outfit. Another good choice is a 10- to 14-foot extension pole that enables you to drop your bait vertically into small openings and lift the fish straight out before they have a chance to wrap your line around a branch.
• **Use light-wire hooks.** Snags are inevitable when fishing in cover this dense. But if you use a long-shank, light-wire hook and relatively heavy line, the shank will usually bend enough that you can pull free.

Important Types of Woody Cover

Brush Clumps. *Brushy cover draws crappies in spring, when high water floods bushes, small trees and other vegetation along the shoreline. Brush that is permanently flooded is less productive.*

Fallen Trees. *Newly fallen trees that have most of their small branches still intact make the best crappie cover. Once the small branches rot away, the cover is less attractive to the baitfish that draw crappies.*

Standing Timber. *Standing trees with plenty of branches for shade and cover make ideal crappie habitat. Under dim-light conditions, the fish suspend high in the trees; when it's calm and sunny, they go deeper.*

Stump Fields. *Common in many reservoirs and some river backwaters, stump fields remain when trees are cut prior to flooding or rot off naturally after being flooded. The bigger the trees, the more attractive the stumps are to crappies.*

Exposed Roots. *Washed-out tree roots can be found along practically any riverbank. Erosion during periods of high water exposes the roots, making superb crappie cover.*

Logjams. *Large trees carried downstream by floodwaters hang up in shallow spots where they continue to catch more logs and debris, eventually creating a logjam. Crappies move into deep holes created by the current swirling around the logs.*

TIGHTLINING IN WOODY COVER

The term tightlining simply means fishing as vertically as possible to minimize snags. You can tightline with a plain jig, a jig and minnow or a jigging spoon. But the most effective setup is a dropper rig baited with one or more minnows (right).

A dropper rig with the sinker at the end of the line and the hooks attached farther up the line is less likely to snag than a slip-sinker rig or any other rig with the hook at the end of the line. With the sinker at the end, you can easily feel the cover and stay just above it. The tandem-hook arrangement also makes it possible to cover a wider depth range.

A tandem-hook dropper rig gives you good vertical coverage.

How to Make a Dropper Loop for a Tandem-Hook Dropper Rig

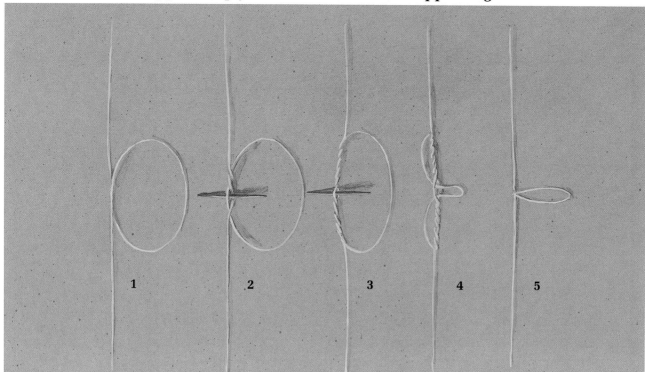

1   2   3   4   5

To make a dropper loop, (1) form a loop in the line, (2) insert a toothpick between the lines, (3) twist the toothpick 4-5 times, (4) remove the toothpick and push the loop through the opening where the toothpick was and (5) snug up the knot by pulling the line on each side of it. Complete the rig by tying a second dropper loop, attaching leaders and light-wire hook using loop-to-loop connections and then adding a 1/2- to 1-ounce bell sinker to the end of the line. The photo at top shows a complete rig.

Tips for Fishing Woody Cover

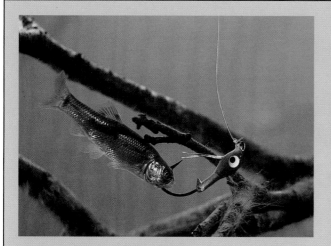

Use a brushguard jig to minimize hang-ups when fishing woody cover. You can buy jigs with plastic, bristle or wire brushguards.

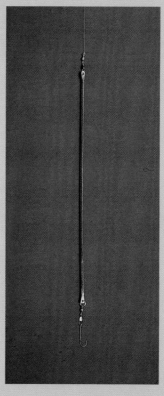

Work a jigging spoon in woody cover by lifting it and then letting it drop on a free line so it flutters erratically. If the lure hangs up, lower your rod tip rapidly; the lure usually pulls itself free when it drops.

Make a "crappie stick" by flattening the ends of a welding rod, drilling holes in the flattened portions and adding small clips to each end. Attach a long-shank light-wire hook to the lower clip. The rod prevents the minnow (or a hooked fish) from tangling your line in the brush. Should you get snagged, just let the crappie stick drop freely; the downward force is usually enough to free the hook.

When fishing in shallow water, unsnag your jig by reeling all the way down to it and pushing it off with your rod tip. You can unsnag a split-shot or slip-bobber rig in the same manner if you crimp the split-shot on lightly so it will slide down the line.

To unsnag your jig in deep water, attach a clip-on sinker to your line and drop the weight vertically. The impact of the weight hitting the jig usually frees the hook. If desired, attach a line to the sinker (shown) so you can drop it again if it doesn't work the first time.

FISHING AT SPAWNING TIME

It's easier to catch crappies around spawning time than at any other time of the year but, even then, it's important to understand early season locational patterns.

The first thing to remember is that not all springtime crappie movements are spawn-related. In early spring,

crappies are drawn to mud-bottom bays, boat canals and other shallow, protected waters that are the first to warm. The warming water draws clouds of baitfish and the crappies move in to feed.

But these early season feeding areas are not necessarily spawning areas, because the

bottom may be too soft for nesting. As spawning time approaches, the fish move to areas with a firmer bottom, usually with brush or some type of emergent vegetation for cover.

If the water is not clear enough to see the crappies, you'll have to fish "blind," methodically working your way through likely spawning areas until you find them. In very dingy water, there probably won't be much in the way of weeds to concentrate the fish, but you may find them holding around stick-ups or brush piles or man-made fish attractors such as "stake beds."

How you fish for crappies around spawning time depends mainly on water clarity and the type of cover the fish are using. Following are some pointers for finding and catching early season slabs.

Approximate Spawning Times of Crappies

Mid May–Mid June

Mid April–Mid May

Mid March–Mid April

Mid February–Mid March

Mid January–Early March

Sight-Fishing for Spawning Crappies

To locate spawning crappies, stand in the bow while your partner slowly motors the boat through a likely spawning area. Be sure to wear polarized sunglasses and keep the sun at your back to minimize glare. If the wind is rippling the surface, however, you may not be able to see the fish. When you spot a crappie, immediately signal your partner to stop the boat. If you're motoring too fast, however, you won't be able to stop the boat before it passes over the fish and spooks them.

Use an extension pole, cane pole or fly rod to drop a jig in front of the crappie's nose. There is no need for a float because you'll be able to see the fish bite.

If you see several crappies, try to catch the darkest ones, which are the males, first. They're much more aggressive than the females and will usually strike the jig immediately.

Fishing "Blind" for Spawning Crappies

Start at the outer edge of the cover—spawning crappies like to have easy access to deep water. Using light spinning tackle and a $1/16$-to $1/32$-ounce jig, cast ahead of the boat as you slowly motor along the outer edge.

After thoroughly working the outer edge, begin working your way farther back into the cover, looking for the thickest clumps of weeds or brush or the most closely spaced stick-ups. If the cover is too thick for a plain jig, try a small spinnerbait.

If you know the location of a man-made fish attractor (such as these wooden structures, which will be dragged to deeper water), work it thoroughly using a slip-bobber rig set to the appropriate depth. Bait up with a minnow.

In natural lakes (dingy or clear), look for crappies in clumps of old-growth bulrushes. The fish usually start to spawn before the new shoots have poked above the surface. Fish any openings in the old bulrush stands using a slip-bobber rig and a minnow.

Tips for Catching Spawning Crappies

Anchor your boat just upwind of a spawning colony (dotted line). You may want to use two anchors to hold the boat sideways to the wind; this way, both anglers can easily reach the fish zone.

When you see crappies, toss out a marker or tie some colored yarn to a branch or sprig of emergent vegetation. The fish may swim away when they see your boat, but they'll usually return in less than a half hour.

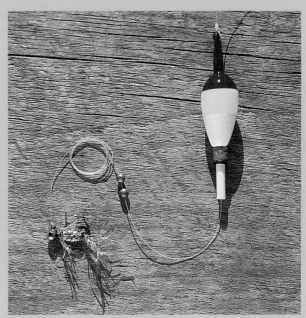

When fishing vertically or using a slip-bobber rig, tie your jig on so it hangs horizontally. This way, it looks like a swimming minnow. If the knot slips to the front of the eye, pull it back to the middle; otherwise, the jig will hang vertically and you'll get fewer strikes.

Use a light-colored jig (preferably white) when sight-fishing. Even in very clear water, it may be difficult to see the fish strike but, with a white jig, you'll see it suddenly disappear so you know exactly when to set the hook.

FISHING IN OPEN WATER

Of all the panfish species, crappies are the least structure-oriented. You know exactly where to find them at spawning time, but they're a lot less predictable the rest of the year. They go wherever they must to find food and don't hesitate to swim far from any kind of structure or cover to feed on zooplankton (or baitfish that are eating the zooplankton) in open water. In most cases, the zooplankton are suspended and so are the crappies.

Most anglers have no idea of where to start looking for crappies in open water, so once the spawning period is over, they focus their attention on other kinds of fish.

Finding and catching crappies in open water can certainly be a challenge, but there are some things you can do to tip the odds in your favor:

• Although the fish may not appear to be relating to anything, they're often within a few hundred yards of a weedline, treeline, rock pile, creek channel or other type of structure to which they can retreat when not feeding.

• Take full advantage of your electronics. Because the fish are often suspended, they are easy to see on a good graph or flasher.

• Remember that crappies in open water are feeding and usually moving, so you must be ready to move with them.

• Pay attention to the wind. Because the fish are relating to plankton concentrations, you're more likely to find them along a downwind shore than an upwind shore.

• Use techniques that give you precise depth control. You can use a slip-bobber rig and a minnow, count down a jig or spinnerbait, "spider-rig" using a variety of lures (p. 52) or vertically jig with a swimming minnow or jigging spoon.

"Prospecting" for Open-Water Crappies

Crappie Zone

Scout for open-water crappies in the zone beginning at the outer fringe of the submergent vegetation to the transition line between hard and soft bottom. You'll also find crappies in a several-hundred yard zone surrounding structural elements such as rock piles and humps.

Before you start fishing, spend some time motoring around areas that you suspect hold crappies. When you see a good-sized school on your depth finder, note their depth and then toss out a marker.

When you're no longer seeing fish on your electronics, motor around your marker in ever-increasing circles until you find them again. After a while, you may be able to establish a movement pattern.

Spider-Rigging

Where fishing with multiple lines is allowed, crappie fishermen use a technique called "spider-rigging." By using anywhere from 4 to 8 rods rigged with lures that run at different depths, they can cover large expanses of open water to locate schools of suspended crappies.

You can spider rig by motoring across a lake, paying no attention to the depth. But you'll normally catch more fish by following a drop-off or working the fringes of cover or structure such as a weedline or rocky hump.

For maximum lateral coverage, use long poles (10- to 12-footers) set in rod holders, preferably those that hold the pole straight out to the side.

Lures for Spider-Rigging

Spinner Fly

Curly Tail Grub

Small Spinnerbait

Bucktail Jig

Slow trolling normally works best, but it pays to vary your speed a little to change the lures' action. Trolling in a loose S-pattern also helps vary the lures' speed and depth, and minimizes spooking by the boat.

Set the poles rigged with the deepest-running lures at the front of the boat; those with the shallowest-running, at the rear. This minimizes the chances of lines becoming tangled as you troll. With the deeper-running lures, your line usually enters the water at a sharper angle; if you set these lines at the rear, they will foul the shallower lines at the front.

Depth-Control Tips

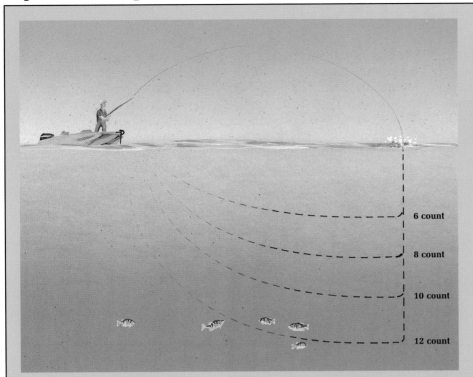

The Countdown Method. *Make a long cast, count as your lure is sinking and then retrieve slowly. Try different counts until you get a strike and then repeat that count on subsequent casts. In the example above, the angler tried counts of 6, 8 and 10 before getting a strike on a 12 count. Don't worry about calculating the running depth based on how fast the lure sinks; let the fish determine the right count.*

6 count

8 count

10 count

12 count

Keep your lure or bait in the upper half of the depth zone the crappies are using. Not only are they are accustomed to looking up for their food, the fish in the upper part of the zone are more active than those in the lower part.

Vertically jig with a Jigging Rap or other swimming-minnow type lure normally used for ice fishing. This presentation gives you precise depth control and, with good electronics, you'll be able to see the lure and the fish.

NIGHT FISHING

There's a very good reason why night fishing for crappies is so popular: Creel surveys have shown that night fishermen often catch crappies at a much faster rate than do those who fish during daylight hours—16 times as fast in one survey.

Night fishing is most effective on clear waters; it is not likely to work well on dingy waters. Although night fishing is most popular in summer, it works well any time of the year, even in winter. In fact, many ice fishermen on northern waters don't even go out until sunset.

In many southern waters, summertime crappie anglers do most of their fishing at night because it's simply too hot to fish during the day. Night fishing is also a good way to avoid excessive boat traffic on heavily used waters.

Finding crappies at night should not be a problem. They're usually in the same areas where you find them during the day, but they're often much shallower. On warm summer evenings, it's not unusual to see crappies dimpling the surface as they feed on emerging insects or baitfish that are feeding on the insects.

Because nighttime crappies are usually suspended well above the bottom, night fishermen rely heavily on their electronics to determine the best fishing depth. As a rule, it's best to keep your bait in the upper part of the fish zone.

By far the most widely used technique for nighttime crappies is still-fishing with a lively minnow beneath a float. Often, anglers use some type of light to draw crappies into the fishing area.

In order to minimize the tangling problems that plague night fishermen, many anglers opt for a cane pole or extension pole instead of a spinning outfit. It's also a good idea to keep an extra rod or pole handy in case such problems develop.

Floating lights, called "crappie lights," emit a beam of light that attracts zooplankton. Crappies move in to feed on the plankton and the minnows that are drawn to the plankton.

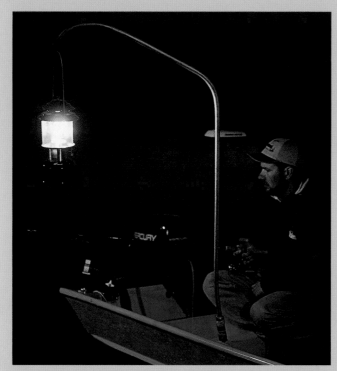

Hang a gas lantern from an arm that extends from the side of your boat. Insects drawn by the lantern help attract crappies, but are a nuisance to anglers. The arm keeps the lantern far enough from the boat that the bugs aren't a problem.

Make a foil hood for your lantern to direct the light into the water. When attaching the hood, make sure you don't cover the air vents beneath the top of the lantern.

Use a lighted float for extra visibility. Rig it to slip by attaching a bobber stop to your line, threading on a small bead and then threading your line through the hole at the bottom. White or fluorescent orange floats are also quite visible at night.

Attach a black (ultraviolet) light to the gunwale of your boat and use fluorescent mono for maximum line visibility. The fluorescent line glows brightly when exposed to the black light.

FLY FISHING FOR CRAPPIES

Although crappies seldom rise to a dry fly, they can easily be taken on wet flies and streamers.

Fly fishing for crappies is most popular in spring, when the fish are patrolling the shallows. Once they go deep in summer, it's difficult to reach them with fly-fishing gear.

If you're intent on fly fishing in summer, be on the alert for surface activity. On warm summer evenings, bug hatches often draw crappies into very shallow water. If fact, you'll sometimes see them swimming about with their backs out of the water, feeding on insects. In most cases, however, they are taking the bugs (or minnows feeding on the bugs) before they reach the surface, explaining why subsurface flies are usually the best choice.

A light fly rod (2- to 5-weight) along with a double-taper or weight-forward line makes a perfect crappie-fishing outfit. Most anglers use a floating line and a 7- to 9-foot leader with a 2- to 6-pound-test tippet. To reach the fish in more than 5 feet of water, however, you'll need a sink-tip line and a 3- to 4-foot leader.

You can also fly fish for crappies using a light spinning outfit with a plastic bubble for casting weight. Or, simply clip a fly onto a small spinner (right). This oldtime method is as effective today as ever.

Popular Crappie Flies

Mickey Finn (streamer)

White Marabou Flash (streamer)

Royal Coachman (streamer)

Black Gnat (wet fly)

Light Cahill (wet fly)

Gold-Ribbed Hare's Ear (nymph)

Aggrevator (streamer)

Fly-Fishing Tips

Side-cast to get your fly to crappies below overhanging branches. Crappies commonly rest in these shady areas, but they would be difficult to reach with spinning gear.

Spin-fish with a wet fly or streamer by clipping it onto a small silver or gold spinner, which provides the necessary casting weight. Or attach the fly to the spinner using a 6- to 12-inch dropper (shown).

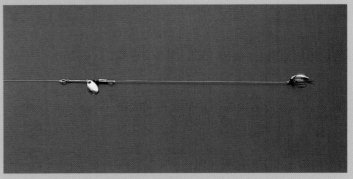

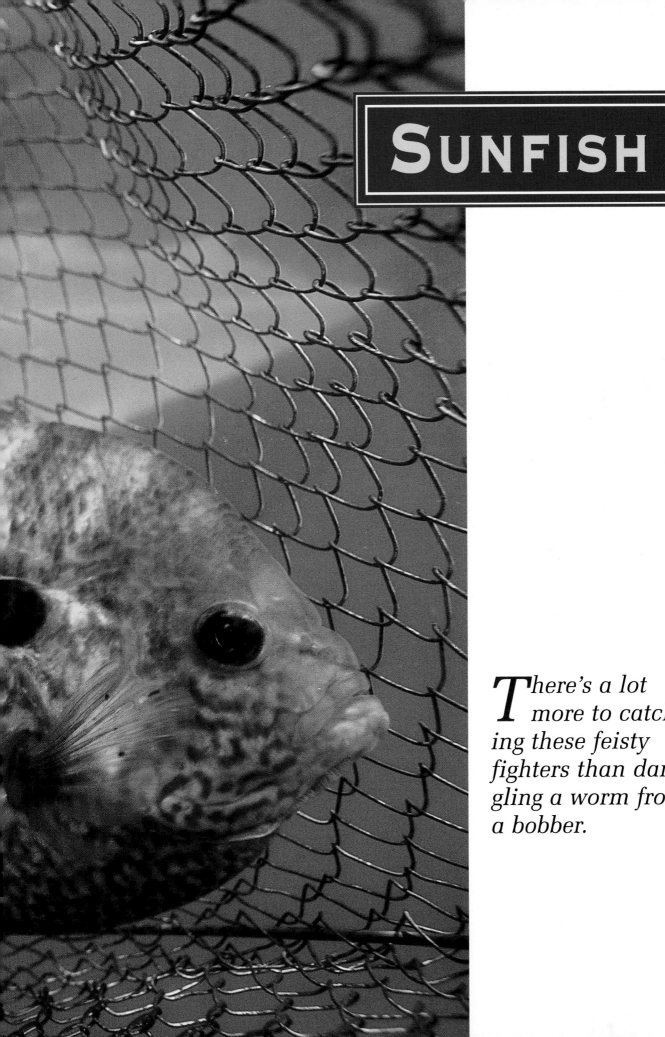

SUNFISH

*T*here's a lot more to catching these feisty fighters than dangling a worm from a bobber.

SUNFISH BASICS

Nobody really knows where the name "sunfish" originated. Some maintain it refers to the bright, sunny coloration of the fish; others say it has to do with the fishes' inclination to bite in sunny weather.

The sunfish family (*Centrarchidae*) includes many of the country's most popular warmwater gamefish, such as largemouth bass, crappies and bluegills. But the term "sunfish" can be confusing, because it also refers to the specific group of centrarchids that are the

which are large enough to draw much angler interest. Two other species, the flier and rock bass, will also be included in this chapter because they not only look like sunfish, they act like them as well.

Like other centrarchids, sunfish are nest builders. The male excavates a spawning bed by fanning the bottom with his tail. The female moves in, the pair spawn and then the male stays on to guard the eggs and later the fry.

Although this parental care ensures good survival of the young, it also leads to a problem that is common among most sunfish species: stunting. When too many of the young fish survive, they compete with each other for food and living space. Their growth rate slows considerably and they may never reach a fishable size.

Compounding the stunting

problem is the fact that most sunfish species are capable of spawning several times over the course of the season. As a rule, the best sunfish waters are those with plenty of predators to keep sunfish numbers in check.

Because two or more sunfish species often nest in close proximity, hybridization is common. Practically every sunfish species interbreeds with every other and, in some waters, it's nearly impossible to find a sunfish that isn't a hybrid. This makes species identification difficult, even for experienced biologists.

The tremendous nationwide popularity of sunfish is easy to understand. They're found in practically every type of warmwater habitat, they're aggressive biters, they're surprisingly strong fighters for their size and they're tops on the dinner plate.

focus of this chapter—members of the genus *Lepomis.* These are the species that anglers commonly call sunfish or, in parts of the South, "bream" or "brim."

There are 11 members of this sunfish group, only 7 of

The extraordinary reproductive potential of sunfish may result in stunting problems.

BLUEGILL

(Lepomis macrochirus)

When you hook a "bull 'gill" and it starts swimming in tight circles and refusing to be pulled in, you'll understand why these feisty fighters are one of America's favorite gamefish.

There are two distinct bluegill subspecies: the northern bluegill and the Florida bluegill (opposite). Regionally popular names for the bluegill include bream, sun perch, sunny and copperbelly.

Bluegills often hybridize with pumpkinseed, green, redear, redbreast and longear sunfish as well as rock bass and warmouth.

You can find bluegills in warm, shallow weedy waters throughout the country. They're most numerous in small, shallow lakes, protected bays of larger lakes and slow-moving reaches or backwater areas of rivers and streams. They prefer water temperatures in the mid- to upper 70s.

Bluegills eat a wide variety of tiny foods including zooplankton, crustaceans, mollusks, fish fry and aquatic insects. Of all the sunfish, bluegills are most likely to take insects on the surface, so they willingly rise to small poppers, sponge bugs and dry flies.

Spawning activity begins in spring, when water temperatures rise into the upper 60s. The fish may spawn at monthly intervals over the

Bluegill Subspecies

Northern Bluegill *(Lepomis macrochirus macrochirus). The edge of the gill cover is light blue, the "ear" is pure black and there is a black blotch at the rear of the dorsal fin. The sides are brownish gold with a purple sheen and may have vague vertical bars.*

Florida Bluegill *(Lepomis macrochirus mystacalis). The back is dark bluish and the sides are lighter with distinct vertical bars. The male (shown) has a copper-colored patch above the eye, accounting for the common name "copperhead." The color of the patch is most brilliant during the spawning period.*

course of the summer, usually around the full moon.

The maximum life span of a bluegill is about 10 years, although few live more than half that long. On the average, it takes about 5 years for a bluegill to reach a weight of ½ pound.

Most bluegills are caught on live bait, particularly worms, leeches, grubs and crickets, but they can also be taken on jigs, spinnerbaits and other tiny artificials.

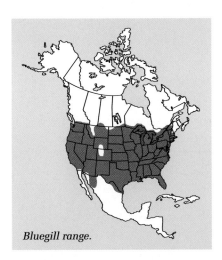

Bluegill range.

World Record: 4 pounds, 12 ounces; Ketona Lake, Alabama; April 9, 1950.

Female bluegills (right) have a yellowish breast. Males (left) have an orange- or copper-colored breast.

REDEAR SUNFISH

(Lepomis microlophus)

Known to most anglers as the shellcracker, the redear is the largest sunfish species. It commonly reaches a weight of 1 pound and 2-pounders are not unusual. In parts of the Southeast, redears are just as popular as bluegills.

The fish get the name "shellcracker" from their habit of eating small snails and clams. In fact, shell beds are prime fishing spots whose locations are closely guarded secrets. Besides snails and clams, the diet includes aquatic insects and many other kinds of invertebrates.

Shellcrackers feed heavily on snails and clams, grinding the shells with pharyngeal teeth in their throat.

Although redears prefer water temperatures in the mid 70s, slightly cooler than that favored by most other sunfish, they cannot live in cold water. This explains why their range does not extend as far north as that of other sunfish species.

Spawning takes place in late spring or early summer, usually at water temperatures in the upper 60s to about 70°F. The beds are normally constructed along the edges of submergent or emergent vegetation. Redears commonly interbreed with bluegill, longear, pumpkinseed and green sunfish.

Redears grow more rapidly than any other sunfish, commonly reaching weights in excess of 1 pound in 5 or 6 years. The maximum life span is about 8 years.

Compared to most other sunfish, redears are harder to catch on artificials. Popular live baits include garden worms, catalpa worms, grass shrimp, crickets and grubs.

They will also eat fish eggs and, on occasion, fish fry. Unlike bluegills, redears seldom feed on the surface.

Redears thrive in clear lakes with moderate weed growth. They're also fond of woody cover, accounting for another common name: "stumpknocker." They're rarely found in current, but they inhabit slack-water pools of rivers and river backwaters. Because they're more tolerant of brackish water than other kinds of sunfish, they're common residents of tidewater rivers.

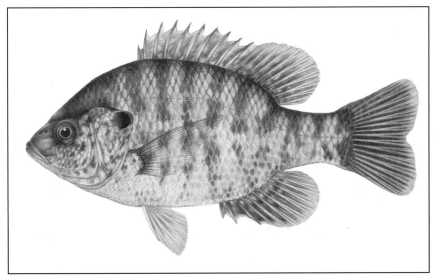

Redear sunfish get their name from the reddish margin around the otherwise black ear. The sides are light greenish or goldish with scattered reddish flecks. There is little difference in coloration between the sexes.

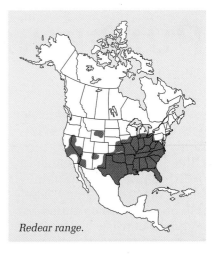

Redear range.

World Record: 5 pounds, 7 ounces; Diversion Canal, South Carolina; November 6, 1998.

PUMPKINSEED
(Lepomis gibbosus)

Some say the pumpkinseed gets its name from its vivid, pumpkin-colored flanks. Others maintain the name is derived from the pumpkin-seed shape of the body. The fish are sometimes called common sunfish, yellow sunfish and "P-seeds."

Pumpkinseeds are one of the most aggressive panfish species, eagerly biting on a wide variety of live baits and artificial lures. Besides worms, leeches, grubs, spin-ners, spinnerbaits and jigs, they will also hit poppers, nymphs and wet flies.

When selecting baits and lures, however, it's important to think small. Pumpkinseeds have a tiny mouth, so if your offering is too large, they'll nibble at it but won't be able to take it. It's also important to use small hooks—no larger than size 8.

Pumpkinseeds favor shallower, weedier water than bluegills or redears. They're most common in small lakes and protected bays of larger lakes. They also inhabit weedy river backwaters and slow-moving stretches of warmwater streams. Because pumpkinseeds prefer water temperatures in the low to mid 70s—cooler than any other sunfish species—their range extends considerably farther north.

Insects (aquatic and terrestrial) are the most important pumpkinseed foods. Other

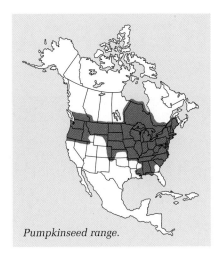

Pumpkinseed range.

Pumpkineeds have orange-gold sides with iridescent blue or turquoise mottling and numerous red or orange flecks. The upper half of the body has 7 to 10 dark vertical bars, which are more noticeable on females. The cheeks are streaked with blue and there is a reddish spot at the tip of the "ear."

World Record: 2 pounds, 4 ounces; North Saluda River, South Carolina; May 26, 1997.

common food items include snails, small crustaceans and fish fry. Like bluegills, pumpkinseeds continue to feed through the winter and are commonly taken by ice anglers.

Pumpkinseeds spawn earlier than bluegills and in shallower water, usually where there is a firm bottom and some type of emergent vegetation. Spawning normally begins when the water temperature reaches the upper 60s. Pumpkinseeds may interbreed with bluegill, green, longear, redear and redbreast sunfish as well as warmouth.

Compared to bluegills and redears, pumpkinseeds grow quite slowly. It generally takes them about 6 years to reach ½ pound. Surprisingly, pumpkineeds in the northern part of the range grow faster than those in the southern part.

Waxworms and other small larval baits are ideal for catching pumpkinseeds.

REDBREAST SUNFISH

(Lepomis auritus)

The redbreast gets its name from the reddish orange breast of the male, which becomes especially intense at spawning time. On females, however, the breast is more yellowish. The greenish sides have red-orange flecks and the cheek has bluish streaks. The black lobe on the gill cover is very long but, unlike that of a longear sunfish, does not have a light margin.

Redbreasts are the most colorful fish that swim in fresh water. Found mainly in rivers and streams along the Atlantic and Gulf coasts and in lakes connected to those streams, they are one of the most current-oriented sunfish species. They're also one of the most salt-tolerant; only the redear can endure more brackish water. Redears prefer water temperatures in the low 80s.

Immature insects, small crustaceans and fish fry comprise most of the redbreast's diet. Primarily bottom feeders, they will occasionally take insects off the surface. They do a fair amount of their feeding at night.

Redbreasts spawn in late spring or early summer, when the water temperature reaches the upper 60s to low 70s. They nest in very shallow water, usually near woody cover. Redbreasts often inter-breed with bluegills, pumpkinseeds, green sunfish and warmouths.

It normally takes about 5 years for a redbreast to reach a weight of $1/3$ pound. They seldom live longer than 6.

Redbreasts will take most of the usual sunfish baits, but they're especially fond of crickets and grasshoppers. They will also strike tiny spinners, fly-rod poppers, wet flies and sponge bugs.

World Record: 2 pounds, 1 ounce; Suwannee River, Florida; April 29, 1988.

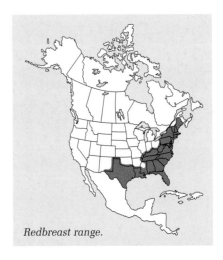

Redbreast range.

LONGEAR SUNFISH

(Lepomis megalotis)

Although the longear is one of the smaller sunfish, it is arguably the most beautiful. The mottling on the sides seems to have a neon-blue glow.

Taxonomists recognize 2 subspecies of longears: The central longear sunfish, which is the largest and most common, and the northern longear sunfish, a tiny fish found only in the southern Great Lakes region.

Like redbreasts, longears are most abundant in moving water. They inhabit clear, gravelly streams with slow current as well as some lakes, ponds and reservoirs. They prefer water temperatures in the upper 70s to low 80s.

Longears eat small crayfish, scuds, snails, fish eggs and fish fry. The best baits are worms, small minnows, crickets, grasshoppers and crayfish. They'll also take tiny spinners, wet flies and nymphs.

Longears spawn later than most other sunfish, usually at water temperatures in the low 70s. They often hybridize with pumpkinseed, bluegill, redear and green sunfish.

The longear grows very slowly, normally reaching a weight of ¼ pound in 5 years. The maximum life span is about 9 years.

Longear range.

World Record: 1 pound, 12 ounces; Elephant Butte Lake, New Mexico; May 9, 1985.

*Longear sunfish have a bright orange background with iridescent blue or turquoise markings on the sides and cheeks. The species gets its name from the long, black gill cover lobe, which has a light margin. The lobe of the central longear (*Lepomis megalotis megalotis, *inset) is longer and more horizontal than that of the northern longear (*Lepomis megalotis peltastes, *main photo).*

GREEN SUNFISH
(Lepomis cyanellus)

Green sunfish have light greenish to brownish sides shading to darker green on the back. The sides have iridescent bluish flecks, accounting for the common name, "blue-spotted sunfish," and the cheeks have bluish streaks. Compared to most other sunfish, the mouth is larger and the body more elongate.

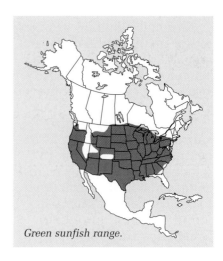

Green sunfish range.

World Record: 2 pounds, 2 ounces; Stockton Lake, Missouri; June 18, 1971.

Despite their diminutive size, green sunfish may well be the most aggressive sunfish species. They'll take on fish many times their size and run them out of their territory. This feisty nature also explains why greens are one of the easiest sunfish to catch.

Green sunfish can tolerate lower oxygen levels than any other kind of sunfish so they can survive in virtually every kind of warmwater environ- ment, including shallow, muddy, stagnant waters that seem better suited to bull- heads. Greens prefer water temperatures in the low 80s.

Insects and small fish com- prise most of the diet, but green sunfish are capable of eating much larger food items. Because of their large mouth, they can easily swal- low foods such as crayfish. Popular baits include worms, leeches, small minnows and tiny spinners.

Green sunfish begin to spawn in late spring or early summer when the water tem- perature reaches the upper 60s or low 70s. They nest in large colonies in very shallow water. Greens interbreed with bluegill, redear, pump- kinseed, longear and red- breast sunfish.

Greens grow quite rapidly, reaching a weight of about ½ pound in 5 years. But they rarely live longer than 6.

Fliers have yellowish green sides with horizontal rows of dark spots. There is a dark vertical bar below the eye. The dorsal fin is very long, with at least 11 spines.

FLIER

(Centrarchus macropterus)

If you catch a fish that looks like a cross between a sunfish and a crappie, it's probably a flier. These small panfish live in shallow lakes, bayous and slow-moving streams in the southeastern United States, but few waters hold large populations.

Fliers are usually found in heavily vegetated waters where they like to hide under mats of floating weeds. They prefer water temperatures from the mid 70s to the mid 80s.

Favorite foods include small crustaceans, insects and fish fry. Fliers are particularly fond of of mosquito larvae and young-of-the-year sun-fish. They readily take worms, grubs and small minnows and will also strike dry flies and tiny poppers.

Fliers spawn earlier in the season than other sunfish. Nesting usually begins at water temperatures in the low 60s. The fish are colony nesters, and anglers who find a spawning concentration can enjoy some fast action.

The growth rate of fliers is highly variable. They grow very slowly in most waters, reaching an average size of only ¼ pound in 6 years. In certain lakes, however, they grow 2 or 3 times that fast. The maximum life span is about 8 years.

World Record: 1 pound, 4 ounces; Little River, North Carolina; August 24, 1998.

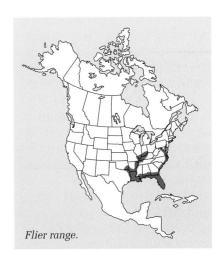

Flier range.

WARMOUTH
(Lepomis gulosus)

The warmouth or "goggle-eye," with its reddish eye and golden-brown sides with dark mottling, closely resembles the rock bass. But it has several dark streaks radiating from the eye, it lacks the horizontal rows of dark spots and the anal fin has only 3 spines instead of 6.

These rock bass look-alikes abound in shallow, weedy lakes and ponds, bayous and slow-moving reaches of streams. Warmouth are more cover-oriented than most other sunfish and are almost always close to dense weeds, brush or timber. They prefer water temperatures in the low to mid 80s and can tolerate temperatures in the low 90s.

Like rock bass, warmouth have a large mouth and an aggressive nature. They feed mainly on small fish, but they also eat insects, crayfish and snails.

In late spring or early summer, when the water temperature rises to the upper 60s, warmouth begin nesting in shallow water with plenty of stumps or weed clumps for cover. You may find them in water only a few inches deep. Warmouth sometimes hybridize with rock bass, bluegill, pumpkinseed, green sunfish and redbreast sunfish.

On the average, it takes about 5 years for a warmouth to reach ½ pound. They live up to 8 years but rarely grow to a weight of more than 1 pound.

You can easily catch warmouth on a worm or minnow beneath a float. They'll also hit small jigs, spinners, wet flies and nymphs, and will rise to tiny fly-rod poppers.

> **World Record:** 2 pounds, 7 ounces; Yellow River, Florida; October 19, 1985.

Warmouth range.

ROCK BASS

(Ambloplites rupestris)

It's a rare day when the rock bass aren't biting. These highly aggressive panfish will take practically any kind of bait or lure that fits into their mouth. Despite their cooperative nature, however, they're not an angler favorite. They're weak fighters for their size and are often infested with parasites, usually yellow grubs.

The name "rock bass" is descriptive because they are commonly found on a rocky bottom. In fact, their latin name, *rupestris*, means living among rocks. The fish are found in a wide variety of natural lakes, reservoirs and rivers, but they're most numerous in clear, weedy lakes and slow-moving streams. They prefer water temperatures in the upper 60s to low 70s.

Rock bass have a varied diet that includes small fish, crayfish, insects, clams and snails. But they do not feed much at water temperatures below 40°F, so they're seldom caught by ice anglers.

Spawning begins in late spring or early summer, when the water temperature reaches the upper 60s. Rock bass usually nest in shallow water in or along the edges of emergent vegetation. They interbreed with warmouth, bluegill and their close relative, the shadow bass.

Rock bass grow at a moderate rate, normally reaching a weight of ½ pound in 6 years. They have been known to live as long as 13.

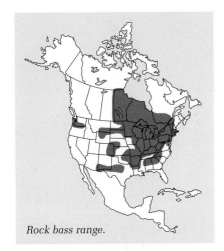

Rock bass range.

World Record: 3 pounds; York River, Ontario; August 1, 1974.

Rock bass have brownish to goldish sides with rows of dark spots and dark blotches along the back. The reddish eye accounts for the common name, "red-eye." Rock bass resemble warmouth, but the anal fin has 6 spines instead of 3. During the spawning period, male rock bass become much darker than females.

WHERE TO FIND SUNFISH

The seasonal movement patterns of sunfish are pretty much the same as those of crappies (pp. 30-33), but their schedule is somewhat different. Because sunfish spawn a little later than crappies, their late spring and early summer movements are delayed as well.

While crappies spawn at water temperatures in the low 60s, sunfish generally prefer temperatures from 5 to 8 degrees warmer. As a result,

they show up on the spawning grounds anywhere from 10 days to several weeks later, depending on latitude and weather. They're also later to show up on the structural elements where they will spend the summer.

The major difference between sunfish and crappies is that sunfish are more cover-oriented. You'll generally find them relating to some type of weedy or woody cover. Although sunfish may

suspend in open water in midsummer or winter, their tendency to roam the middle depths is not as great as that of crappies.

Another important difference: Sunfish will tolerate brighter light than crappies so they usually stay a little shallower and are not as likely to retreat to deep water on a calm, sunny day. It's not unusual to catch sunfish in a few feet of water under the midday sun.

How To Catch Panfish

Sunfish Location in Natural Lakes During...

Early Spring
- Shallow mud-bottom bays that warm earlier than the main lake.
- Man-made boat canals.
- Boat harbors.
- Patches of dead weeds along sheltered shorelines (in bowl-lakes with no distinct bays).

Man-made boat canals.

Boat harbors.

Spring (spawning)
- Shallow bays and harbors with a sandy or gravelly bottom.
- Sheltered sandy or gravelly shorelines.
- Gradually sloping points with new-growth emergent

Flooded trees.

vegetation.
- Around the bases of flooded trees in shallow water.
- Around shallow-water docks.

Docks in shallow water.

Summer and Early Fall
- Points and inside turns along irregular weedlines.
- Underwater lips of shoreline points.
- Edges of weedy humps.
- Suspended in open water.
- Around deep-water docks.
- Scattered over deep weed flats.
- Over shell beds (redears).

- Around flooded trees in deep water.

Deep-water dock.

Underwater lip of point.

Late Fall and Winter
- Shallow bays just after freeze-up.
- Deep holes in shallow bays.
- Deep holes in shallow parts of the main lake.
- Sharp-sloping points.
- Steep portions of breaklines.
- Inside turns along weedlines.

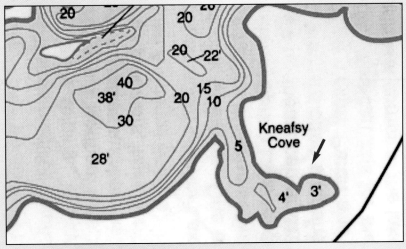

Shallow bay after freeze-up.

Sunfish Location in Man-Made Lakes During...

Early Spring through Spawning
- Points at mouths of creek arms.
- Back ends of creek arms, particularly those with clear water.
- Secondary creek arms.
- Marinas.
- Gradually tapering points in creek arms.
- Shallow, brushy flats along creek channels.
- Brushy main-lake coves.

Summer and Early Fall
- Main-lake humps.
- Extended lips off points in main lake and deep creek arms.
- Edges of main river channel.
- Edges of creek channels.
- Intersections of creek channels. and the old river channel.
- Edges of old road beds.
- Around man-made fish attractors.

Late Fall and Winter
- In old stock ponds or lake basins.
- Deep holes at mouths of creek arms.
- Deep sections of creek channels and old river channel.
- Off deep main-lake points.
- Deep main-lake coves.

Brushy flat.

Protected cove with plenty of cover.

Man-made fish attractor.

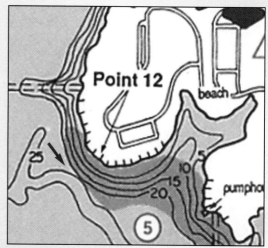

Deep main-lake point.

Sunfish Location in Rivers During...

Early Spring through Spawning
- Eddies below low-head dams.
- Eddies below boulders or other current breaks.
- Emergent vegetation along shorelines with little current.
- Shallow sandbars.
- Shallow, weedy backwaters.
- Stump fields in backwaters.

Late Spring to Early Fall
- Brushy cover along the edge of the main channel.
- Eddies or slackwater zones with weedy cover.
- Deep back-waters with weedy or woody cover.
- Around deep boulders.
- Along riprap banks with slow-moving water.
- Around piers and breakwaters.
- On weedy wingdams with slow current.

Late Fall and Winter
- Shallow backwaters just after freeze-up and before ice-out.
- Deep, slack-water holes in main channel.
- Deep outside bends in main channel.
- Deep holes in backwaters or connected oxbow lakes.

Backwater with weedy or woody cover.

Eddies and slackwater zones below boulders or current breaks.

Riprank bank with slow-moving water.

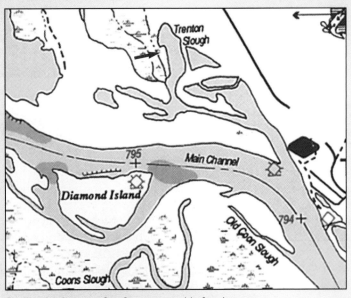

Shallow backwater after freeze-up and before ice-out.

SUNFISHING BASICS

Depending on your point of view, angling for sunfish can be the easiest kind of freshwater fishing—or the most difficult.

If you're content to catch a mess of quarter-pound sunnies, you can set up an easy chair on most any dock and haul in enough to feed the whole family. But if you're targeting sunfish pushing a pound, your challenge is as great as that of any trophy bass, walleye or pike fisherman.

Here's some general advice for boosting your odds of catching good-sized sunfish:

• **Fish deeper.** There will be times when you'll find big sunfish in shallow water, especially during the spawning period, but they normally frequent deeper water than the smaller sunfish.

• **Use good electronics.** Finding schools of sunfish in expanses of deep water is nearly impossible without good electronics. Before dropping your line, spend some time scouting likely structure with your graph or flasher. Sunfish are easy to see because they rarely hold tight to the bottom.

• **Keep moving.** Sunfish are more mobile than you may think. There's no guarantee that the spot where you caught fish yesterday will hold a single fish today. But when they move, they usually don't go far; check a productive spot thoroughly before giving up on it.

• **Fish during peak times.** Although sunfish will bite at any time of year, the best time to catch big ones, hands down, is during the spawning period. You know exactly where to find the fish and they're more aggressive than at any other time of the year. Luckily for anglers, most kinds of sunfish spawn two or three times over the course of the summer, usually at monthly intervals and often during the full moon.

You can catch sunfish throughout the day, particularly in dingy waters, but they normally bite best early and late in the day. Some kinds of sunfish, such as the redbreast and longear, are commonly caught after dark.

• **Know your species.** A technique that works well for one species of sunfish may not be as effective for another. Bluegills, for example, are prone to surface feeding and, when conditions are right, will eagerly take poppers, sponge bugs and other topwaters. Redears, on the other hand, are primarily bottom feeders, so fishing with surface lures would be a waste of time.

• **The right tackle.** As in crappie fishing, many sunfishermen make the mistake of using tackle that is too light. Ultralight gear and 2-pound-test mono are fine for those quarter-pounders in light cover, but a plate-sized bluegill in a bulrush bed will make short work of equipment that light. In that situation, you need a medium-power spinning outfit or an extension pole with 8- or even 10-pound-test mono.

Your odds of catching big sunfish are best at spawning time. The fish are on their beds, and they'll hit most anything that comes close.

Natural Baits

When the sunfish are biting, you can catch them on most any kind of small natural bait. In fact, there are times when they'll grab a bare hook. But those occasions are rare; the fish are usually more discerning and at times are downright finicky. You may have to experiment with several baits to see what the fish want on a given day.

Of all the panfish, sunfish are the most scent-oriented. If the bait doesn't smell right, they may ignore it. That explains why fresh, lively bait will usually outproduce dead bait. Of course, the big sunfish are a lot more choosy than the small ones.

Natural bait may not be necessary in warm weather, when the fish are aggressive. But it's a major plus when the water is cool or the fish are turned off because of a cold front or other adverse weather condition.

Different kinds of sunfish have different bait preferences. Most sunfish species have tiny mouths, so you'll need fairly small baits. It's possible to catch a big sunnie on a whole nightcrawler, for example, but you'll catch a lot more on a half crawler or even an inch-long piece.

Serious sunfishermen generally use extra-long-shank bait hooks. If you're using a short-shank hook and a sunfish swallows the bait, as they often do, you'll have a hard time removing the hook from its small mouth and will probably kill the fish. Long-shank hooks also work well for threading on insect baits and hooking worms several times so only the tail is left dangling.

Natural baits are commonly used for tipping tiny jigs, spinners and other small artificials. And some fly fishermen add a bit of worm to their hook to draw more strikes.

Popular Sunfish Baits

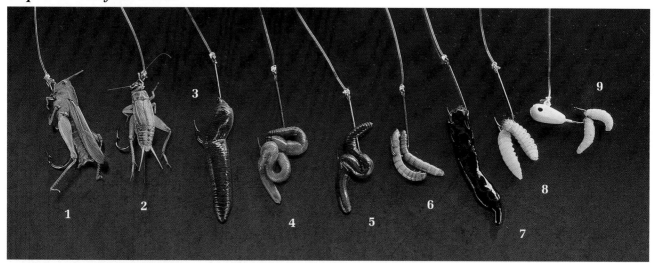

Popular sunfish baits include: (1) grasshopper; (2) cricket; (3) nightcrawler half; (4) garden worm; (5) red wiggler; (6) mealworms; (7) small leech; (8) waxworms; (9) spikes; (10) grass shrimp; (11) catalpa worm.

Popular Sunfish Lures

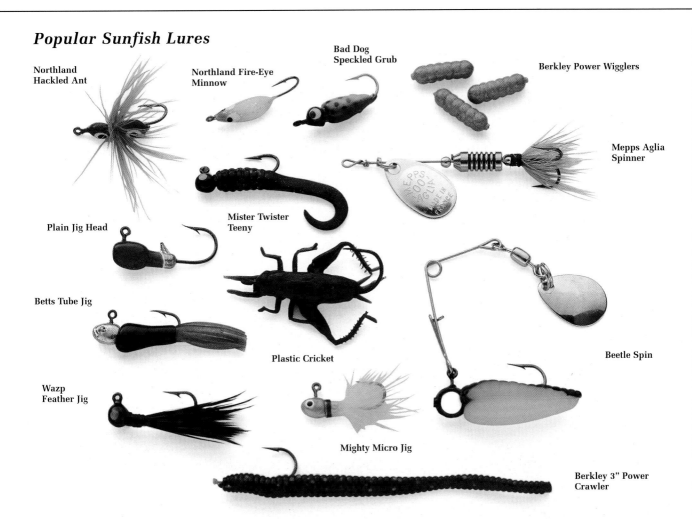

Northland Hackled Ant

Northland Fire-Eye Minnow

Bad Dog Speckled Grub

Berkley Power Wigglers

Mepps Aglia Spinner

Plain Jig Head

Mister Twister Teeny

Betts Tube Jig

Plastic Cricket

Beetle Spin

Wazp Feather Jig

Mighty Micro Jig

Berkley 3" Power Crawler

Artificial Lures

With the notable exception of fly fishermen, few sunfish enthusiasts use artificial lures—unless they're tipped with live bait.

But it definitely pays to carry a selection of artificials. They enable you to cover expansive weedbeds and brushy flats that would be difficult to fish any other way. And when the fish are really turned on, you can catch them faster on lures because you don't have to waste time baiting your hook.

One of the most effective sunfish lures is a $\frac{1}{16}$- to $\frac{1}{32}$-ounce curlytail jig. The tail has an enticing wiggle that appeals to most sunfish. Marabou jigs also work well as do plain jig heads tipped with small pork strips, scent-impregnated fabric or live bait.

Tiny spinnerbaits ($\frac{1}{16}$ to $\frac{1}{8}$ ounce) have their place in sunfish angling as well. They have enough lift that you can retrieve them slowly over the weedtops, and their safety-pin shaft keeps them weed-free even when you work them through the vegetation. They also work well for straining open water to find suspended sunfish, as do ordinary in-line spinners.

An increasing number of anglers are now using ice-fishing lures for catching sunfish in the warm-weather months. These lures are usually, but not always, tipped with some type of grub.

Other effective lures include realistic soft-plastic insect imitations and tiny plastic worms fished on a split-shot rig.

Fly-fishing lures and techniques are covered on pages 96-97.

A tear-drop tipped with a small grub works as well in summer as in winter.

FISHING IN WEEDY COVER

Sunfish are the most cover-oriented panfish species and, of all the possible cover types, weeds are their favorite. They use a wide variety of weed types including submergent, emergent and floating-leaved varieties.

Compared to crappies, sunfish are much more likely to hold right in the weeds, rather than along the edges. You'll seldom find them right in clumps of closely spaced plants, however—they're more likely to be in the pockets between the clumps.

Waters with light to moderate weed growth are usually a better choice than those with very dense weeds. Heavy weed cover protects too many of the small sunfish from predators, so they tend to over-populate the habitat and become stunted.

The condition of the weeds is important as well. Healthy green weeds usually draw more sunfish than dead or decaying weeds. In fact, when the weeds start to die off in fall, you can often find sunfish concentrated in the remaining clumps of green weeds.

How you fish sunfish in weedy cover depends on the type of weeds they're using. Here are the types of vegetation most commonly used by sunfish and some strategies for fishing them.

Techniques for fishing in emergent weeds will be covered in "Fishing at Spawning Time" (pp. 90-93).

Weeds Commonly Used by Sunfish

Submergent Weeds. Broad-leaved submergent plants, such as "cabbage," provide better sunfish cover than narrow-leaf varieties. The broad leaves offer shade and visual concealment.

Emergent Weeds. Used primarily during the spawning period, emergent plants such as bulrushes and maidencane may also hold sunfish in summer, if the plants grow in deep enough water.

Floating-Leaved Weeds. Lily pads and other floating-leaved plants provide a canopy of overhead cover, yet have enough open space underneath that sunfish can swim about freely.

Slop. A mat of floating-leaved plants, submergent plants and filamentous algae makes good summertime cover because it keeps the water beneath it a few degrees cooler.

How Weather Affects Sunfish Location

Where you find sunfish in the weeds depends, to a large extent, on the weather. On warm, still, humid days, the fish are likely to be swimming high in the weeds or working the edges (left). On cold-front days, they'll be buried much deeper in the weeds (right).

Fishing in Floating-Leaved Weeds & Slop

When you're fishing in scattered lily pads or other loosely spaced surface vegetation, you can cast and retrieve a slip-bobber rig, jig, spinnerbait or practically any of the usual sunfish offerings. But when you're faced with an almost solid blanket of floating-leaved weeds with only a few scattered openings, you really have no choice but to use a long pole and drop your bait vertically into the holes.

Even if you could cast accurately enough to hit an opening, you would have little chance of reeling in a fish without losing it. With a long pole, you can hoist the fish out vertically before it can tangle in the vegetation.

How to Fish with a Long Pole

Set up a cane pole or extension pole so the line (10- to 14-pound-test mono) is about the same length as the pole. If your line is too long, you won't be able to control it well enough to swing the bait into a tight spot. Attach a small float and set it to the appropriate depth.

Gently swing the rig into a nearby opening; it should alight gently to avoid spooking the fish. If you don't get a bite within 15 seconds or so, pick up your bait and swing it into another opening. After trying all the openings you can comfortably reach, reposition your boat and repeat the process.

Tips for Fishing Dense Surface Vegetation

A shaking lily pad is a signal to gently drop your bait as close to the pad as possible. The shaking is usually caused by a sunfish picking bonnet worms off the bottom of the pad.

If the vegetation is so dense that you can't find an opening, make one using a garden hoe. The disturbance usually dislodges insects from the weeds and draws sunfish into the area.

Fishing in Submergent Weeds

It's difficult to fish right in submergent vegetation. Unless the water is very clear or the weedtops grow nearly to the surface, you normally can't see the weeds well enough to place your bait in the openings.

But when sunfish are actively feeding, there is no need to fish right in the weeds. The fish are more likely to be along the edges of the weeds or over the weed-tops, opening the door to numerous fishing methods.

A light spinning outfit spooled with 6-pound-test mono is a good choice for fishing in most types of sub-mergent vegetation, but a long pole works better in shallow weedbeds, where the open-ings are visible.

How to Fish Shallow Submergent Weeds

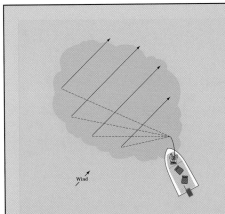

Work a shallow weed flat by setting a slip-bobber rig to keep the bait just above the weedtops. Cast upwind and let the rig float down-wind of your position, varying the angle of successive casts to cover all water within casting distance.

Motor slowly over a deep weed flat or along a weedline, looking for schools of sunfish on your depthfinder. When you spot some fish, toss out a marker. Try casting to them. Or, repeatedly slow-troll over the area using a slip-sinker rig.

How to Fish Deep Submergent Weeds

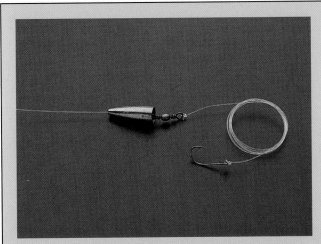

Make a slip-sinker rig for fishing in weedy cover using a 1/8- to 1/4-ounce bullet sinker for weight. If necessary, peg a corkie or other small float to your line about a foot above the hook to keep your bait riding above the weeds.

Motor slowly over a deep weed flat or along a weedline, looking for schools of sunfish on your depth finder. When you spot some fish, try cast-ing to them or repeatedly slow-troll over the area using a slip-sinker rig.

FISHING IN BRUSHY COVER

Any kind of woody cover will hold some sunfish, but newly flooded brush with the small branches still intact is more attractive to most kinds of sunfish than large trees or old brush with most of the fine branches rotted away.

Sunfish are most likely to find suitable brushy cover in man-made lakes and rivers. When a reservoir is first filled, sunfish have a virtually unlimited supply of flooded brush. But over time, this cover gradually deteriorates

to the point where it holds very few sunfish. You'll still find some good brush, however, along eroding banks where trees tumble into the water and on shallow flats with seasonally flooded bushes. Most rivers have a good

supply of brushy cover in the form of washed-out tree roots, tops of fallen trees and logjams.

Brush piles make excellent cover for spawning sunfish, but they hold plenty of sunfish at other times of the year as well. The brush provides shade, shelter from the current and a source of food. Good brushy cover usually has plenty of aquatic insects and crustaceans clinging to the branches and small baitfish hiding between them.

In waters where little brushy cover exists, anglers commonly make their own brush piles from Christmas trees or bundles of tree limbs (where legal), creating "private" fishing holes. Conservation agencies may also put out brushy "fish shelters."

The options for fishing in brushy cover are limited.

When the sunfish are active, you may be able to draw them out of the cover with jigs, spinnerbaits or flies, but most anglers prefer to go in after them.

A long pole rigged with 10- to 14-pound-test mono comes in handy for dropping your bait into small openings in the brush and poking it under the bank or into other tight spots that would be tough to reach by casting.

Good Brush Versus Poor Brush

Good Brush. *Most of the fine branches are still intact, providing sunfish with food and cover. The longer the brush is submerged, the more of the fine branches that rot away.*

Poor Brush. *If the brush has been submerged for many years, few of the fine branches remain, so there is far less little substrate for insects and crustaceans and less cover for sunfish.*

Tips for Fishing in Brushy Cover

Use a long pole to poke your bait beneath an undercut bank or into other hard-to-reach spots. Pull the float tight against the rod tip to get it under the bank, then release the line and pull the pole back out.

Use a slip-bobber rig and a small jig tipped with natural bait when fishing in brushy cover. Then, should you get snagged, you can pull the line tight and then push the rod tip down to dislodge the jig.

The most common way to find sunfish in small streams is to "jump" woody cover. Methodically work your way along the stream channel, using a long pole to drop your bait into fallen trees, brush piles, logjams and any other likely cover.

RIVER FISHING

If you're looking for an untapped sunfishing opportunity, check out some of the warmwater rivers and streams in your area. Few anglers think of rivers and streams as prime sunfish waters, but many offer surprisingly good fishing, particularly for redbreasts, longears and greens, and sometimes for bluegills. Some tidal rivers are known for their top-rate shellcracker fishing.

Most streams have an abundance of sunfish cover including fallen trees, brush piles, logjams, undercut banks, washed-out roots and deep pools. Big rivers have all the same cover types plus brushy side channels, weedy backwaters and an abundance of man-made cover like wingdams and riprap banks.

When planning your river-fishing strategy, it's important to consider water-level fluctuations. For example, sunfish often move into shallow backwaters when the water is rising, but they move out when it's falling. They respond to water-level changes of only an inch or two.

Water-level fluctuations also affect sunfish location in streams with lots of weedy or brushy cover along the banks. Rising water draws the fish far back into the weeds or brush where they can get out of the current and feed on insects clinging to the vegetation. If the cover is dense, it may be nearly impossible to get your bait to them. Falling water, on the other hand, pushes the fish to the outer edges of the weeds or brush where you can reach them more easily.

This pattern is most noticeable on tidal rivers. Knowledgeable sunfish anglers prefer to do their fishing around low tide, when the fish are concentrated along the outer weed edges.

How Water Levels Affect Sunfish Location in Rivers

Rising Water. *Sunfish move into the shallower water and denser cover near shore. The higher the water the farther into the cover they will go.*

Falling Water. *Sunfish move out of the shallow, dense cover into deeper water nearby.*

Other Stream-Fishing Methods

Anchor within easy casting distance of the bank and drift a slip-bobber rig along the outer edge of weedy or brushy cover along the channel margins.

Wade small streams that would be impossible to fish with a boat. Cast a slip-bobber or split-shot rig into eddies and deep pools. If possible, wade upstream so the silt kicked up by your feet doesn't drift over the fish.

Drift downstream, casting to weedy or brushy cover using a tiny spinnerbait tipped with a piece of worm or other live bait.

FISHING AT SPAWNING TIME

Compared to most other gamefish, sunfish spawn over a much longer period, giving fishermen a prolonged opportunity to enjoy the fast action.

Weeks before spawning gets underway, sunfish begin to congregate in shallow bays, coves, channels, boat harbors and backwaters that warm earlier than the main body of water. Although the fish move into these areas to feed on invertebrates and small baitfish, they may stay there to spawn if they can find an area with a firm bottom and suitable weedy or brushy cover.

If there are no acceptable spawning sites in these early-season areas, the fish will move into the main body of water to spawn. They often choose a spawning site around the mouth of a bay or cove.

As a rule, the clearer the water, the deeper you'll find the spawning beds. In dingy water, they may be as shallow as 6 inches; in gin-clear water, as deep as 15 feet.

Early in the spawning season, you'll find a preponderance of small males on the spawning grounds. The females and larger males may not show up until several days or weeks later.

In clear water, you can find sunfish beds by motoring through the weedy shallows, looking for light-colored depressions. If you see some nests (or some fish), use the same sight-fishing methods as you would for crappies (p. 47). If the visibility is poor, you'll have to fish your way through a potential spawning area to find the beds. Be on the lookout for swirls, wakes or any other fish movement in the shallows; it might be an indication of spawning activity. If you catch a male sunfish that is "peeing," you know that the spawn is underway.

Some veteran redear and

Approximate Spawning Times of Sunfish

Late May–Late June

May

April

March–Early April

February–March

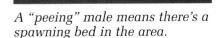

A "peeing" male means there's a spawning bed in the area.

bluegill fishermen claim they can find the spawning beds by sniffing for them. They describe the odor as fishy or cucumber-like.

Once you find a spawning area, be sure to carefully note its location. Sunfish return to the same spawning areas year after year, so they'll most likely be back on the same spot in seasons to come.

The Spawning Sequence

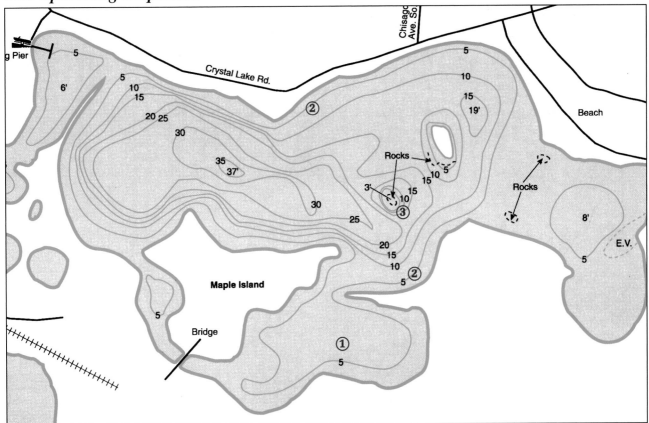

Sunfish begin to spawn at different times in different parts of the same body of water. Spawning activity starts earliest in (1) shallow bays, because these areas are the first to warm. Spawning activity along (2) the main lakeshores usually gets underway 7 to 10 days later and spawning on (3) humps and other mid-lake structure usually begins yet another week later.

Look for spawning sunfish in new-growth bulrushes. The tips of the plants usually reach the surface when the water temperature reaches the upper 60s, the same temperature at which most kinds of sunfish start to spawn.

Check openings in emergent weeds or brush to find spawning sunfish. Seldom will you find beds among the dense weed growth.

Sunfish often nest beneath tree branches, roots or other types of overhead cover that offers shade and protection from predatory birds.

Sunfish nest in deeper water as the season progresses. The year's first spawn (1) is usually in shallow, weedy water on a shoreline flat; the next spawn, in deep weeds (2) on a gradual break; the final spawn, in water as much as 15 feet deep at the outer edge of the weeds (3).

Tips for Catching Spawning Sunfish

Watch for ripples, swirls, wakes or other movements that could reveal the presence of spawning sunfish.

If sunfish refuse to bite on a bobber rig, remove the float (inset) and drag your bait right over the spawning bed. The fish will attack anything they think is a threat to the nest.

If you find a spawning bed and catch a few fish on it in midday, return and try it again just as the sun is setting. Spawning activity picks up around dusk and many more fish move into the bedding area.

Work the deep outer edges of the spawning area to catch the biggest sunfish. As a rule, you'll rarely find the big ones in water where you can see the bottom.

POND FISHING

Many anglers have the idea that ponds produce only small sunfish, but the record books prove otherwise. Nearly half of all the current state and line-class records for the major sunfish species came from some type of pond or mine pit.

Although the majority of ponds—and most of the best ones—are on private property, that doesn't necessarily mean they're off limits. If you ask them, many pond owners will grant you permission to fish. Others will allow you to fish for a small fee.

The extra hassle required to gain access to a private pond is well worth the effort. The reason these waters produce so many big sunfish is that they receive considerably less fishing pressure than most public waters.

There are many different kinds of ponds, most of them man-made. They range in size from a fraction of an acre to more than 10 acres, but the majority fall into two categories: Bulldozed ponds and dammed ponds (opposite).

Fishing a pond is not much different than fishing any

other small lake. The secret is finding the best cover and structure along with suitable water temperatures and oxygen levels.

What many anglers fail to consider, however, is that many fertile ponds do not have enough oxygen in the depths to support sunfish in summer. If a pond does not have an inlet and outlet, it may stagnate in hot weather, so the sunfish are forced to stay in the shallows even though the depths offer cooler water.

Types of Man-Made Ponds

Bulldozed Ponds. These ponds are usually round or rectangular, with a bowl-shaped basin. The deepest water is in the center. They are fed by runoff rather than a permanent flow, so there is little mixing and the water stratifies into temperature layers in summer. The deepest water may not have enough oxygen to support sunfish.

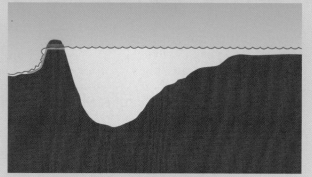

Dammed Ponds. Created by building an earthen dam across a small stream, a pond of this type usually is deepest at the base of the dam. In some cases, there is a deep trench at the base of the dam where fill was removed to build the structure. Because of the moving water, ponds of this type seldom stratify into temperature layers.

Pond-Fishing Tips

Use a float tube to fish structure in the middle of a pond. The deep creek channel running through many ponds often holds the biggest sunfish, for example, but there would be no way to reach it from shore.

Look for sunfish around the mouths of inlets (arrow). In spring, sunfish congregate around inlets because they carry in warmer water. In summer, inlets draw sunfish because they offer cooler water.

In dammed ponds, work the deep hole at the base of the dike to catch sunfish in midsummer. Use a slip-bobber rig and experiment with different depths.

FLY FISHING FOR SUNFISH

When sunfish are slurping insects off the surface, even some of the most avid "big game" fishermen grab their fly rods to get in on the fast action.

To most anglers, fly fishing for sunfish means catching bluegills on small poppers. Bluegills are the most surface-oriented of the sunfish species and, when an insect hatch is in progress, the fish attack practically any small fly that floats. Most other sunfish will take flies on the surface as well, although redears are much more likely to feed on the bottom.

Some anglers think that the only time to catch sunfish on poppers, sponge bugs and other surface flies is during the spawning period. With so many sunfish in the shallows, that is certainly one of the best times, but it's not the only time. Surface flies also work well on warm days in early spring and on warm summer evenings.

You don't hear as much about sunfishing with subsurface flies, but it can be equally effective. The main advantage to subsurface flies (wet flies and nymphs) is that they catch fish whether or not a hatch is in progress.

If you're not a fly fisherman, don't be intimidated by the thought of picking up a fly rod. Sunfish are much less discriminating than trout, so you don't have to make picture-book casts and perfect retrieves to catch them. In fact, fly fishing for sunfish is a good way to learn the basic fly-fishing skills that can later be applied to other kinds of fish.

It doesn't take an expensive, custom-made fly rod to catch sunfish. You can buy a decent fly-fishing outfit for about the same price as a good spinning outfit. Refer to pages 9 to 11 for information on selecting fly-fishing gear.

Popular Sunfish Flies

Bugs

Sponge Bug

Popper

Dry Flies

Blue Quill

Royal Coachman

Brown Spider

Wet Flies

Black Gnat

Hare's Ear Soft Hackle

Comet

Fly-Fishing Tips

Listen for the characteristic "smacking" sound made by a sunfish sucking an insect off the surface. That's your cue to tie on a popper, sponge bug or dry fly.

Cast directly to the rise; your fly should set down right on the spot where you saw the fish. If you cast beyond the rise and your line slaps down right on top of it, you'll probably spook the fish.

Use a weighted wet fly or nymph to catch sunfish on the spawning beds. Nest-guarding males may be reluctant to rise to a surface fly, but they will aggressively attack a fly pulled over the nest.

YELLOW PERCH

Catching small perch isn't much of a challenge, but it takes some more refined techniques to consistently bag "jumbos."

YELLOW PERCH

(Perca flavescens)

Highly prized as a table fish, the yellow perch is one of the country's most popular panfish species. Lakes that produce "jumbo" perch (those weighing ¾ pound or more) draw hordes of anglers. In many waters, however, the perch are too small to interest fishermen, but the tiny fish make excellent forage for walleyes, bass, pike and many other large predators.

Although several other unrelated panfish species are called "perch," yellow perch are the only true perch, because they belong to the perch family (*Percidae*).

Yellow perch are close relatives of the walleye and sauger, but they do not have the fanglike teeth and their eye lacks the reflective pigment that gives the walleye and sauger excellent dim-light vision.

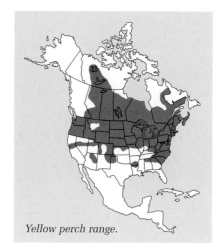

Yellow perch range.

Yellow perch have bright yellowish sides with 6 to 9 dark vertical bars, accounting for their common names "raccoon perch" and "ringed perch." The lower fins often have an orange tinge and are bright orange on spawning males. Perch have a pair of dorsal fins; the front dorsal has spiny rays; the rear, soft rays.

World Record: 4 pounds, 3 ounces; Delaware River, New Jersey; 1865.

Considered coolwater fish, yellow perch favor water temperatures from the mid 60s to low 70s. The biggest perch come from good-sized lakes with moderate depth, clarity and weed growth. They are usually found in open-water areas with a firm bottom. Perch also inhabit smaller lakes and ponds as well as warmwater streams with medium to slow current. They have been stocked extensively in the South.

Yellow perch are daytime feeders. Their diet consists mainly of small fish and immature aquatic insects such as mayfly larvae, which they root out of the bottom mud. They also eat fish eggs, crayfish, small clams and snails. Perch are particularly fond of scuds, or "freshwater shrimp," and fertile lakes with a large scud crop produce some of the biggest perch.

Spawning takes place shortly after ice-out, usually at water temperatures in the mid 40s. After dark, the fish drape long gelatinous strands of eggs over weeds, fallen branches or debris in shallow water. The parents do not guard the eggs or young.

Yellow perch have been known to live up to 10 years, but their usual life span is 6 years or less. Their growth rate varies considerably, depending mainly on the predator-prey balance. In many waters, perch are so numerous that they become stunted and rarely reach a length of more than 6 inches. Jumbo-perch lakes usually have a large population of walleyes, northern pike or other predator fish to keep the perch population in check.

The best perch waters have plenty of predators to thin out the perch population.

WHERE TO FIND YELLOW PERCH

You can find small perch most anywhere—the trick is finding the big ones. It's unusual to find jumbo perch in small lakes or streams, so we will concentrate on locational patterns in large natural lakes.

Before we discuss specific seasonal locations, however, there are a few things you should keep in mind in your search for big perch:

• Jumbo perch are bottom-oriented. Unlike small perch they seldom suspend in open water to feed on plankton. Start fishing on or near the bottom but keep an eye on your depth finder because there will be times when the big perch move up to feed on suspended baitfish.

• You can find big perch over practically any kind of bottom. They often comb sandy or gravelly bottoms to find tiny clams or snails and they're also drawn to rock piles with plenty of small crayfish. But they're just as as likely to root around in a soft, muddy bottom to find larval insects such as mayflies or midges.

• Jumbo perch are not necessarily associated with structure. You'll often find them roaming over large flats, blocks from any type of structure or cover.

This means that you can't really predict where the fish will be on a given day, so you must be willing to do a lot of exploring.

• Don't be afraid to go deep. Although perch are commonly found in the thermocline, they may go well below the thermocline if that's where the food is. In many large natural lakes, anglers catch perch at depths of more than 30 feet in both the summer and winter months.

Yellow Perch Location in Natural Lakes

Early Spring through Spawning
- Shallow bays with light weed growth.
- Tops of sand-gravel points.
- Protected shoreline flats with sparse weeds.
- Tops of shallow rocky reefs and gravelly humps.
- Around mouths of inlets.
- Around piers and breakwaters.

Late Spring to Early Fall
- Irregular shoreline breaks.
- Extended lips of points.
- Edges of humps.
- Mud flats surrounding humps.
- Sand-gravel flats.

Late Fall and Winter
- Sharp shoreline breaks.
- Deep rock piles and gravel bars.
- Sharp breaks off long points.
- Deep humps.
- Mud flats surrounding deep humps.
- Sand-gravel to mud transitions.

Shallow bay with light weeds.

Sparsely-weeded shoreline flat.

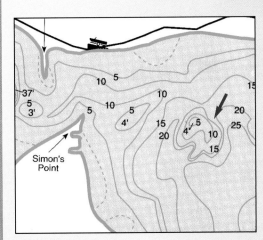

Edge of hump.

Deep rock piles and gravel bars.

PERCH-FISHING BASICS

Perch have a reputation for being willing biters—in fact, some would say they're downright stupid. But there's a big difference between those tiny perch that constantly nibble at your bait and the jumbos.

When conditions are just right, jumbo perch are just as aggressive as the little ones. But more often, they're a lot fussier. Here are some pointers for outwitting the finicky jumbos:

• **Slow and steady.** Big perch will seldom chase a fast-moving bait; they're more likely to study it for awhile and then swim over to take a tentative nip at it. Only rarely do they bite with much conviction.

This means that a slow presentation usually works best. Either still-fish or try drifting or trolling at the slowest speed possible. If you're jigging, the action should be subtle rather than intense.

through dozens of tiny perch in hopes of catching a jumbo—it rarely happens.

• **Capitalize on perches' competitive nature.** Perch have an interesting habit that many anglers have learned to use to their advantage. If you've ever reeled up your bait and seen hundreds of perch following it, you know that the fish can be extremely competitive. The big ones don't compete for food as aggressively as the small ones, but it's possible to draw a scattered school into a small area and work them into a feeding frenzy.

One productive tactic is still-fishing with several closely-spaced lines. The concentration of baits draws the fishes' interest and when you hook one, the struggle seems to "turn on" other members of the school. The action starts slow but soon escalates into a non-stop bite. As long as you keep some baits in the water, the perch will stick around. To further increase the intensity of the action, you can chum the area by tossing pieces of minnows or other bait.

• **Light tackle.** Yellow perch are not strong fighters and are seldom caught in snaggy cover, so there is really no need for heavy tackle. A light spinning outfit with 4- to 6-pound-test mono will work nicely for most perch fishing.

• **Fish deep.** You can catch small perch in shallow water, deep water or anywhere in between. The big ones move into the shallows to spawn in spring and may return to feed in fall, but they're found in relatively deep water most of the year.

• **Be willing to move.** Perch tend to school by size. If you're catching nothing but small ones, you need to move. It doesn't pay to weed

Jumbo perch inspect the bait closely before taking it.

Natural Baits

Natural bait accounts for the vast majority of yellow perch but, when it comes to selecting bait, there is really no clear-cut favorite. In some regions, the majority of anglers rely on minnows while in others, leeches or night-crawlers get the nod. And many veteran perch fishermen will tell you that nothing compares to a wig-gler (mayfly larvae). Wigglers, they say, will catch even the fussiest perch. Other popular perch baits include crickets, small crayfish, cray-fish tails and a vari-ety of larval baits such as waxworms and spikes (mag-gots).

Small baits will improve your hooking percentage.

In selecting perch baits, the usual wisdom is to think small. Perch have a relatively small mouth and are reluctant to tackle large baits. Even if they do, you probably won't hook them.

Here's a trick that could save the day if you run out of bait. Poke the eyeball out of a perch you've already caught. Put it on a plain hook or use it to tip a tiny jig or jigging spoon. A small strip of belly meat is also a good choice. Be sure to check your state's reg-ulations to make sure these baits are legal.

Popular Perch Baits

Popular natural baits for perch include: (1) minnow; (2) garden worm; (3) nightcrawler half; (4) small crayfish; (5) crayfish tail; (6) perch belly; (7) perch eye; (8) mayfly wiggler; (9) waxworms; (10) cricket; (11) small leech.

Artificial Lures

Because jumbo perch are so bottom-oriented, it's not surprising that they're easily caught on lead-head jigs. Just about any kind of small jig will do the job, but it's hard to beat curlytails and marabous in ⅛- to ¹⁄₁₆-ounce sizes. The tiny jig/grub combos used in ice fishing for perch also work well at other times of the year, but they're so light that you'll have to add split-shot or fish them beneath a float.

Another highly effective perch lure is a small (⅛- to ¼-ounce) jigging spoon tipped with a minnow head, perch eye, small leech or piece of worm. When jigged vertically on the bottom, a spoon kicks up puffs of mud that attract the perch.

Perch fishermen also use a variety of spinners. When the

Perch are drawn to the puffs of mud kicked up by a jigging lure.

fish are in weed-free shallows, try a plain in-line spinner with a size 0 or 1 blade. When they're on a shallow flat with scattered weeds, a ⅛-ounce spinnerbait is a better choice. For trolling or drifting in deep water, use a spinner/live-bait rig.

Some anglers use tiny spoons and crankbaits for catching perch in expanses of open water but, in most cases, these lures serve mainly as locational tools.

As a rule, perch prefer bright colors such as fluorescent chartreuse or orange. In fact, some anglers attach bright-colored flags to their anchor ropes to attract perch.

Popular Perch Lures

Genz Worm Tipped with Waxworms

Little Cleo

Mister Twister Meeny

Blue Fox Minnow Spin

JB Lures Tadpole Spin

Northland Buck Shot Rattle Spoon

Lindy Fuzz-e-Grub

Spinner & Minnow Rig with a Slip-Sinker

FISHING IN SHALLOW WATER

One of the best times to catch jumbo perch is in early spring, when they congregate in bays and along protected shorelines to spawn. But most anglers miss out on the action because they don't get out early enough. By the time the weather warms up and most other gamefish start to bite, perch fishing is winding down.

In northern waters, perch move into their spawning areas shortly after ice-out. When the water temperature reaches the mid 40s, they drape their egg strands over old plant stems, brush, logs or rocks, usually in water less than 6 feet deep.

If you like easy fishing, you'll love catching spawning perch. They'll hit just about any kind of small bait or lure you put in front of them, and they don't seem to mind if there's a boat hovering right over them.

If the water is clear enough, you can sight-fish for perch using the same technique as you would for crappies (p. 47). Using a long pole and 6- to 8-pound-test mono, just dangle a $\frac{1}{16}$- to $\frac{1}{8}$-ounce jig a few inches in front of the fish. As in crappie fishing, the females are not as aggressive as the males, but you may be able to entice them to bite by adding a small minnow to the jig or rapidly jiggling it (below).

Where you can't see the fish, try fancasting with a small jig or spinner to locate them and then, once you've found them, switch to a float and a minnow or other live bait. The secret in fishing with a float is to set your depth to keep the bait within inches of the bottom. Unlike crappies, jumbo perch are reluctant to swim up more than a foot or so to take the bait.

You can catch a few good-sized perch in the spawning areas for a week or two after spawning has been completed. But by the time the water temperature reaches the low 50s, most of the jumbos have retreated to deeper water.

They will return to the shallows in early fall, beginning when the water temperature drops into the 60s. Use the same techniques as you would in spring, particularly on warm, sunny days when the shallows are teeming with baitfish.

Big-lake fishermen catch lots of perch off piers and breakwaters in early spring and in fall. The fish are drawn to the riprap facings of these structures.

Tips for Catching Shallow-Water Perch

Hang your jig in the face of a perch and jiggle it rapidly; the fish usually strike as the jig is settling to rest.

Use a dropper rig (p. 44) for pier fishing. Tie a ½-ounce bell sinker to the end of the line and add several droppers at 1- to 2-foot intervals. Bait up with small minnows. Because the droppers are ahead of the sinker, you'll notice even the lightest taps.

FISHING IN DEEP WATER

Once perch have abandoned their inshore spawning sites and scattered into deeper water, locating and catching them may be a challenge. You're faced with a basic dilemma: You have to cover a lot of water to find the fish, but you can't use fast-moving lures because perch usually ignore them.

Further compounding the problem is the fact that perch are difficult to locate with your electronics because they tend to hug the bottom more closely than most other gamefish.

There will be times when perch are holding on breaklines around points, humps or reefs, but they could just as easily be scattered over a flat, muddy bottom, feeding on insect larvae.

To locate perch, troll or drift slowly along a breakline or across a flat using a slip-sinker rig, a spinner rig, a jig tipped with live bait or a small spoon or crankbait. Watch your electronics closely to spot any perch schools; when you see some fish or start catching them, drop a marker.

If the perch are scattered over a large area, continue trolling or drifting. If they're tightly schooled, anchor your boat just upwind of the school and toss out a slip-bobber rig set to keep your bait just inches off the bottom. By fishing with several slip-bobber rigs in the same small area, you may be able to work the school into a feeding frenzy. While you're pulling in fish on one line, the other lines are still in the water to keep the perch interested. Another good outfit for catching tightly schooled

Good electronics are a must for finding deepwater perch.

perch is a spreader rig (below).

A GPS unit is invaluable for deep-water perch fishing. Should you find a big school of perch over a mayfly bed in the middle of nowhere, you precisely mark the spot and return another day.

How to Make & Use a Spreader Rig

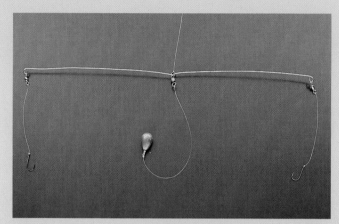

Wrap a 14- to 18-inch piece of stiff wire around the middle of a large barrel swivel and add smaller barrel swivels to loops on the ends. Tie a foot-long mono dropper with a 1-ounce bell sinker to the middle swivel and 6-inch droppers with size 4 hooks to the ends.

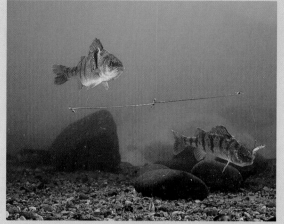

While anchored or drifting very slowly, lower the spreader rig vertically. When the sinker touches the bottom, the baits will be a few inches above the bottom. When you feel a tap, set the hook; you'll often have a pair of perch.

Tips for Catching Deep-Water Perch

Save your dead minnows and use them for chumming your fishing spot. Periodically toss a few minnow pieces into the water to hold perch in the area and keep them feeding aggressively.

Slow your drift speed by using a sea anchor or "drift sock." This keeps your bait moving slowly enough that perch will take it. You can also use a drift sock to slow your trolling speed.

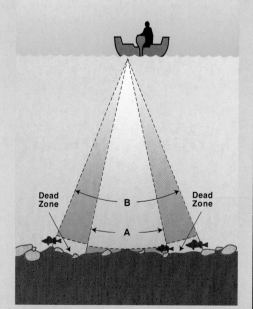

Your transducer should have a narrow cone angle so you can spot bottom-hugging perch. A narrow cone (a) has a very small "dead zone" compared to a wide cone (b).

TEMPERATE BASS

It's possible to catch these aggressive feeders by the hundreds, if you know when, where and how.

TEMPERATE BASS BASICS

All temperate bass have a quality that endears them to anglers: They are, without a doubt, the most aggressive feeders that swim in fresh water.

Temperate bass are known for their "pack feeding" habits. A school of bass surrounds a pod of baitfish or herds them into a bay or other area where there is no escape. The bass furiously slash into the hapless baitfish, eating as many as they can before the pod breaks up. The frenzied feeding may last for just a few minutes and then the school moves on to find another baitfish pod.

When you're on one of these pack-feeding schools, you can catch a fish on every cast. But the very behavior that makes the fish so easy to catch makes them difficult to find. They roam open water, sometimes far from any kind of structure or cover, and even when you do locate a big school, the action is usually short-lived.

Striped bass, the largest member of the temperate bass family (*Moronidae*), may reach a weight of 60 pounds or more. All the other freshwater members of the family (with the exception of white perch) bear a striking resemblance to the striper, with a silvery coloration and dark horizontal stripes along the sides. But they seldom reach a weight of more than a pound or two, so they are considered "panfish."

Temperate bass are classified as warmwater fish, favoring water temperatures above 70°F. They are also known as "true bass" as opposed to largemouth bass and other "black bass" which are actually members of the sunfish family.

Temperate bass differ from black bass in that they are random spawners rather than nest builders. The eggs are deposited in moving water and allowed to drift with the current. When conditions are right, tremendous numbers of the eggs hatch, resulting in enormous year-classes that provide outstanding fishing a few years later. But most temperate bass have a relatively short life span, so the bounty is fleeting.

Look for circling and diving gulls (they're going after injured baitfish) to locate a school of temperate bass.

WHITE BASS

(Morone chrysops)

If you like fast action, try fishing for white bass when they're concentrated on their spawning grounds or tearing into schools of baitfish in open water. It's not unusual to catch hundreds of them in a day of fishing.

Like other members of the temperate bass family, white bass feed in packs. They often surround schools of open-water baitfish, such as shad and emerald shiners, and herd them to the surface. It's not unusual to see white bass

boiling the water over an area of several acres. Whites also eat crustaceans, immature aquatic insects and a variety of other small baitfish. They'll feed at any time of the day, but they're normally most active around dusk and

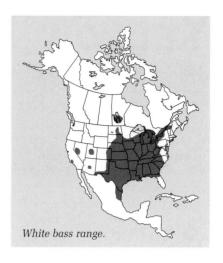

White bass range.

White bass (often called silver bass or sand bass) have silvery sides with black horizontal stripes that are unbroken above the lateral line but broken in an irregular pattern below. The body is deeper than that of a striped bass and there is a single patch of teeth on the tongue, rather than two patches. The dorsal fins differ from those of a yellow bass in that they are not joined at the base, and the lower jaw is considerably longer than the upper.

World Record: 6 pounds, 7 ounces; Saginaw Bay, Michigan; September 19, 1989.

dawn. In clearwater lakes, they commonly feed at night, especially during the summer months.

In spring, when the water temperature reaches the upper 50s or low 60s, huge schools of white bass swim upriver to spawn below a dam or other migration barrier. They deposit their eggs on sand-gravel shoals with light current and then abandon them. Lake-dwelling white bass spawn on sand-gravel shoals or at the mouths of tributary streams. White bass hybridize naturally with yellow bass. Striped bass-white bass hybrids, called *wipers*, are produced in hatcheries and stocked throughout the southern U.S.

The best times to catch white bass are in spring, when they congregate to spawn, and in late summer and fall, when they begin pack-feeding in open water.

You can easily catch white bass on small minnows, but live bait is seldom necessary.

Artificials about the same size as the predominant baitfish will usually do the job. Jigs or other lures with a single hook enable you to unhook the fish quickly and get back into the water while the bite is still on.

White bass thrive in reservoirs, big rivers or natural lakes connected to rivers. They prefer water temperatures from the mid 60s to mid 70s. Although they're most numerous in southern waters, particularly those with an abundance of open-water forage, their range extends into southern Canada.

White bass usually reach a weight of 1 to 1½ pounds in their normal 5- to 6-year life span. But 2- to 3-pounders are common in some waters. They seldom live longer than 6 years.

Wipers have stripes that are broken above and below the lateral line. The body is deeper than that of a striper but not as deep as that of a white bass.

YELLOW BASS

(Morone mississippiensis)

If you're like a lot of other anglers who fish the Mississippi River and its connecting waters, you've caught yellow bass but you may not even know it. These scrappy fighters bear a close resemblance to their cousin, the white bass, but they have a yellowish rather than silvery hue.

Sometimes called "barfish" or "streakers" because of the heavy dark stripes on their sides, yellow bass are primarily a southern species, although they can be found as far north as southern Minnesota and Wisconsin. While they're confined primarily to the Mississippi River and its larger tributaries, they're more abundant in backwaters, connecting lakes and impoundments than in main-channel habitat. They prefer large, weed-free expanses of open water and water temperatures in the upper 70s.

Although yellow bass are by no means rare, finding a body of water with good numbers of them may be a challenge. Biologists have long puzzled over the fact that yellow bass abound in certain lakes or rivers while dozens of similar waters in the same area have practically no yellows.

A weedy river backwater is a favorite yellow bass hangout.

Like white bass, yellow bass are pack-feeders, but they are much less inclined to feed on the surface. They may herd baitfish into the shallows, but more commonly they feed in midwater or on the bottom. Besides shad and other small fish, their diet includes zooplankton and immature aquatic insects. Yellow bass feed most heavily around dawn and dusk, but sporadic feeding continues throughout the day.

In spring, yellow bass swim upriver or into tributary streams to spawn. When the water temperature reaches the upper 50s or low 60s, they scatter their eggs on gravelly shoals. They may also spawn in shallow shoal areas of lakes. The parents do not protect the eggs or fry. The fact that yellow bass often share their spawning areas with white bass explains why the two species sometimes hybridize.

Yellow bass may live as long as 7 years, but few survive longer than 4. At that age, they usually weigh ½ to ¾ pound.

Yellows will never be as popular as whites, but they have a cadre of loyal followers. Although they're harder to find and don't grow as large, they have firm, flaky white meat that most anglers will tell you is better eating. You can catch yellows on small jigs, spoons and spinners. When they're fussy, you'll need live bait, usually worms or minnows.

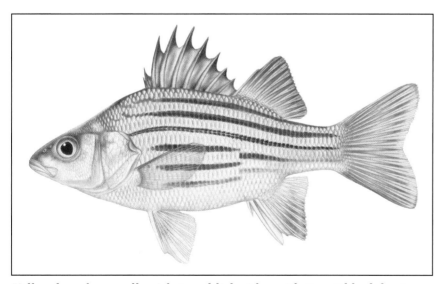

Yellow bass have yellowish to goldish sides with 6 or 7 black horizontal stripes that are very distinct. They resemble white bass, but the stripes below the lateral line are broken on a slanted line just ahead of the anal fin, the dorsal fins are joined at the base and the lower jaw protrudes only slightly beyond the upper.

Yellow bass range.

World Record: 2 pounds, 4 ounces; Lake Monroe, Louisiana; March 27, 1977.

WHITE PERCH

(Morone americana)

White perch may be the least known of all the panfish species. Like their much larger cousin, the striped bass, they can tolerate fresh, brackish or salt water. Some white perch spend their entire life in fresh water while others are anadromous, living at sea and then entering rivers along the Atlantic coast to spawn. The latter are often called "sea perch."

Because they belong to the temperate bass family, white perch are not really perch at all. Their name is somewhat confusing, because some anglers use the name white perch when refering to crap-pies and sheepshead (freshwater drum).

White perch are found in a variety of habitats including warm, shallow lakes and reservoirs, tidal rivers and their estuaries and even warmwater bays of the Great Lakes. They prefer water temperatures in the upper 70s.

The diet changes from season to season. In spring, white perch feed primarily on immature aquatic insects, especially mayfly nymphs. By summer, young-of-the-year baitfish have grown to an acceptable size, so they become the primary forage. But the baitfish soon become too large for the perch to swallow, so they switch back to aquatic insects and crustaceans such as freshwater shrimp.

Although white perch will pack-feed on the surface when the opportunity presents itself, they are less prone to this type of feeding than are white bass. They may feed sporadically throughout the day, but they're most active around sunset or after dark.

White perch spawn in spring, usually at water temperatures in the low 50s. Anadromous perch swim into estuaries, scattering their eggs

White perch range.

White perch, sometimes called "silver perch," have silvery to grayish green sides with no horizontal stripes. The back is brownish or blackish.

in the main channel, tributaries or small ditches flowing into tributaries. Lake-dwelling populations usually spawn in inlets. The parents do not protect the eggs or fry. White perch have been known to hybridize with striped bass.

The usual life span of a white perch is 5 to 7 years, although some live as long as 15. They commonly reach a weight of about 1 pound in 7 years, but seldom grow much larger. In fact, many waters have stunted populations with few fish ever reaching ½ pound.

Most white perch are taken on worms and minnows, but small artificials also work well. Spinners, spoons, jigs and small minnowbaits are popular with spin-fishermen; wet flies and small streamers with fly anglers.

For most of the year, white perch are fish of open water.

WHERE TO FIND TEMPERATE BASS

All temperate bass, with the exception of anadromous or marine forms, have similar seasonal movement patterns. They winter in deep portions of a lake, reservoir or river and then migrate toward their spawning areas in spring. The migration begins at water temperatures in the mid to upper 40s, with males arriving on the spawning grounds several days before females.

As spawning time approaches, huge numbers of fish stack into small areas, meaning can't-miss fishing for anglers who find the right spots. The fish continue to bite right through the spawning period, which gets underway at water temperatures in the 50s.

After spawning, the fish scatter and may be difficult to find. White bass and, to a lesser extent, yellow bass and white perch, are constantly on the move in search of open-water baitfish. Fishing improves greatly in late summer and fall, however, as the fish begin to pack-feed on schools of young-of-the-year baitfish.

The action slows in late fall as baitfish pods break up and the fish retreat to deeper water. In some lakes and reservoirs, they spend the winter in massive schools.

If you're lucky enough to find one of these wintering concentrations, you'll enjoy non-stop action, even at near-freezing water temperatures. In big rivers, tremendous numbers of fish crowd into warmwater discharges from power plants.

Temperate Bass Location in Rivers During...

Early Spring through Spawning
- Backwaters and marinas that warm earlier than the main river.
- Tailwaters of upstream dams.
- Eddies in main channel below tailwaters.
- Mouths of large tributaries.
- Estuaries of tidal rivers (white perch).
- Tributaries flowing into tidal estuaries (white perch).

Deep riprap banks.

Late Spring to Early Fall
- Sandy flats around mouths of tributaries.
- Pools with rocky feeding riffles just upstream.
- Deep riprap banks along outside bends.
- Slots and washouts below boulders and other large objects that break the current.
- Eddies created by sharp turns in the river.
- Eddies created by points projecting into the river.

- Tributaries flowing into tidal estuaries (white perch in fall).

Late Fall and Winter
- Deepest holes in main river channel.
- Deep outside bends.
- Deep washouts in the tailwaters of upstream dams.
- Deep sections of main channel of tidal estuaries (white perch).
- Around warmwater discharges from power plants.

Backwaters.

Warmwater discharge areas.

Temperate Bass Location in Reservoirs and Natural Lakes During...

Early Spring through Spawning
- Tailwaters of upstream dams.
- Creek arms at the upper end of the lake, particularly those with a significant flow.
- Mouths of inlet streams (natural lakes).
- Shallow bays (natural lakes).

Late Spring to Early Fall
- Edges of shallow flats.
- Mouths of major creek arms.
- Suspended over the old river

Edges of large sand flats.

channel and creek channels or in the submerged timber along the edges.
- Along edges of shallow main-lake points.
- Along edges of large sand flats.
- Narrows between main-lake basins.

Late Fall and Winter
- Deep holes at mouths of creek channels.

- Junction of creek channel and old river channel.
- Deep holes in the old river channel at the lower end of the lake (late fall to early winter).
- Deep holes in the old river channel at the upper end of the lake (late winter).
- Deep main-lake points, especially those at the upper end of the lake.
- Along edges of large sand flats.

Tailwaters.

Mouths of creek channels.

FISHING FOR TEMPERATE BASS

Fishing for temperate bass is a feast-or-famine proposition: One day you'll haul them in like a TV fishing star; next day, you can't buy a bite. These erratic results can be explained by the fishes' nomadic behavior. They roam huge expanses of water in their continual search for food. And even when you do cross paths with them, the encounter is usually of short duration.

Many anglers fish for temperate bass only during the spawning period, because that's the time when the fish are most predictable. But that's a big mistake. If you take the time to familiarize yourself with their habits, you can can catch plenty of fish at other times of the year as well. Here are some tips for improving your consistency:

• **Cover lots of water.** Temperate bass are not hard to catch, they're just hard to find. If you plant yourself in a spot that recently produced with the idea of "waiting them out," you'll probably be waiting a very long time. Instead, use trolling tactics to locate the fish and be willing to move as soon as the action stops.

If you start catching small fish, keep moving. Temperate bass tend to school by size and it's unlikely that there will be any big fish mixed in with the small ones.

• **Be a bird watcher.** Gulls and terns have an uncanny ability to quickly pinpoint schools of pack-feeding bass.

Many baitfish are injured during the feeding melee, and the birds can evidently spot them struggling on the surface from blocks away. When you see a flock of birds circling, screeching and diving into the water, get to the spot in a hurry.

• **Don't spook them.** When you locate some feeding bass, don't run your boat right into the school. You'll spook them and they'll be gone in seconds. Instead, stop well short of the school and make long casts.

• **Vary your depth.** Temperate bass may feed on the surface, on the bottom or anywhere in between. Even when you see them slashing at baitfish on the surface, it's possible that there are even more fish a few feet down.

• **Fish at peak times.** Temperate bass are usually more active early or late in the day than in the middle of the day. In clearwater lakes, they may feed through the night. As a rule, fishing is best in stable weather, especially when skies are overcast or there is a little wind to ripple the surface and reduce light penetration.

• **Don't be undergunned.** Temperate bass are powerful fighters for their size. Most anglers use light- to medium-light spinning gear with 6- to 8-pound-test mono. You could get by with ultralight gear in most situations, but then you would have to fight the fish longer and risk spooking the entire school.

When handling temperate bass, don't grab them by the gills. The gill cover has a razor-sharp spine (arrow) that can inflict a painful wound.

Lures & Baits for Temperate Bass

Day in and day out, no lure or bait catches more temperate bass than a leadhead jig. You can fish it shallow for surface feeders, count it down when they're in midwater or hop it along bottom when they're deep. And when you find an aggressive school, the single hook enables you to unhook the fish quickly and get your line back into the water. Most anglers prefer ⅛- to ¼-ounce jigs including curlytail, marabou, bucktail, feather-tail and horsehead models.

But there will be times when other lures will work as well or even better. A tailspin, for example, is an excellent choice when you need to make long casts to reach a surface-feeding school. You can reel it steadily to catch the fish that are up high or let it helicopter to reach deeper

It's important to use a lure that matches the size of the predominant baitfish present where you're fishing.

Popular Live Baits & Lure-Bait Combos

Lindy Fuzz-e-Grub Tipped with Minnow

Grass Shrimp

Blue Fox Super Vibrax Tipped with Worm

Angleworms gobbed on a hook

Spinner & Nightcrawler Rig

Popular Lures for Temperate Bass

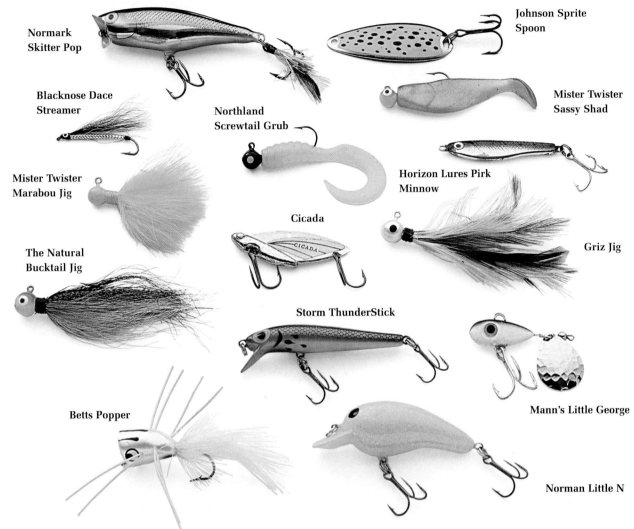

Normark
Skitter Pop

Johnson Sprite
Spoon

Blacknose Dace
Streamer

Northland
Screwtail Grub

Mister Twister
Sassy Shad

Mister Twister
Marabou Jig

Cicada

Horizon Lures Pirk
Minnow

Griz Jig

The Natural
Bucktail Jig

Storm ThunderStick

Mann's Little George

Betts Popper

Norman Little N

Fathead Minnow Hooked
Through Back

fish. A tailspin is also a good choice for vertically jigging in deep water, as is a bladebait or jigging spoon.

When the fish are scattered, try trolling with a crankbait, minnowbait, spoon or spinner rig to locate them and then switch to a jig.

Fly fishing with flashy minnow-imitating streamers works exceptionally well when the fish are feeding in shallow water. When they're surface feeding, they'll also hit small poppers.

When selecting lures for temperate bass, remember that size and shape is much more important than color and action. When the fish are

feeding on young-of-the-year shad only about an inch long, for instance, they won't pay much attention to a 3-inch crankbait. But they'll greedily attack a $\frac{1}{16}$-ounce jig tipped with a tiny shad-tail or curly-tail grub.

Live bait is seldom necessary to catch temperate bass, although there are times when it's more effective than artificials. When white perch are rooting insect larvae out of the bottom, for example, a garden worm or grass shrimp will usually outproduce any artificial lure. Live bait also works well in clearwater lakes, in cold water or under cold-front conditions.

FISHING AT SPAWNING TIME

With tremendous numbers of fish congregated in a very small area and feeding aggressively, the spawning period offers the year's fastest temperate bass action. But the timing is critical because the peak bite lasts only a week or so.

You can time the bite by paying close attention to the water temperature. The fish begin migrating toward their spawning areas at water temperatures in the upper 40s, but the huge spawning concentrations don't develop until water temperatures reach the mid to upper 50s.

You may also be able to time these runs based on the runs of other more popular fish. In rivers where anglers focus primarily on walleyes, for example, the white bass generally start showing up about the time the walleye bite is winding down.

The very best place to catch spawners is in the tailwaters of a dam that blocks the spawning run. Major dams are found on virtually all big rivers and reservoirs. Smaller dams or "low-head" dams are prevalent on smaller rivers, many of which are the primary spawning streams for lake-dwelling populations of temperate bass.

But you can also catch the fish in pools, eddies, backwater lakes and marinas along the way to the spawning grounds. The fish will tolerate light current but are seldom found in swift current.

In reservoirs, many temperate bass spawn in the back ends of creek arms that have a significant inflow, or on sand-gravel shoals at the upper end of the lake, especially in years when the flow of the main river is lower than normal.

Spawning concentrations are much harder to find on natural lakes that have no major inlets, but some fish may congregate around the mouths of small tributaries.

Although the majority of spawners are caught by boat fishermen anchored in these key locations, the spawning run gives shore fishermen a better chance to catch these fish than they will have at any other time of the year.

Casting with small jigs, spinners or spoons accounts for most of the fish, but fly fishing with flashy streamers is also popular in some areas.

The white bass spawning run means exciting fishing and fast action.

Tips for Finding and Catching Spawners

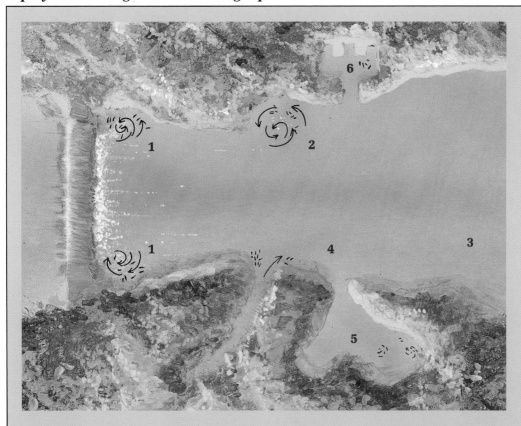

During the spawning period, look for temperate bass (1) in eddies in tailwater areas, (2) in eddies along the edge of the main channel, (3) in slack-water pools in the main channel, (4) around mouths of tributaries, (5) in shallow backwater lakes and (6) in marinas.

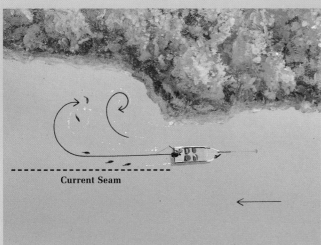

Fish an eddy by anchoring your boat so that its back end is at the eddy's upstream end. This way, you can retrieve your lure along the current seam (dotted line) and easily reach the rest of the slack-water zone.

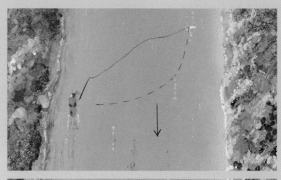

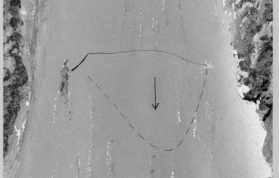

Fly-fish for temperate bass in slow current by angling your cast upstream and (top) then stripping in line fast enough to prevent the current from sweeping your fly too far downstream and causing "drag" (bottom).

FISHING IN OPEN WATER

No matter what the conditions, pinpointing temperate bass schools is a challenge. And it's even more difficult when those schools are scattered over vast expanses of open water.

Luckily for anglers, the fish often provide some visual clues to help solve the locational puzzle. When schools of temperate bass are herding baitfish, for instance, you'll often see swirls and splashes and you may even be able to spot baitfish (usually shad) jumping out of the water to escape the hungry predators.

If there are gulls and terns in the area, they'll spot the surface activity long before you do and will lead you to the action.

The technique of spotting these surface-feeding schools, working them until they sound and then finding another school is called "jump-fishing" (below). Jigs, preferably with flattened barbs (p. 132), are the best choice for jump-fishing because you won't have to waste time trying to dislodge treble hooks.

When there is no apparent surface activity, the best way to locate the fish is to troll for them. Just toss out a small plug, spoon or jig and motor over a flat or along a breakline. You can cover a wide swath of water and a range of depths by spider-rigging (p. 52).

Should you start catching fish, stop the boat and try casting or vertically jigging with leadheads or tailspins. If the fish are deep, you may be able to work the school for quite a while before it breaks up or moves away.

One thing to remember when scouting for temperate bass in open water: They like to trap the baitfish by pushing them up against a steep ledge or into a dead-end bay. This explains why a breakline that drops sharply into deep water is better than one with a gradual slope.

Jump-Fishing for Temperate Bass

Use binoculars to search for gulls or terns diving into the water to feed on shad injured in the feeding melee. Make sure the birds are actually diving, not just flying around.

Get to the spot in a hurry, but stop well short of the school. If you motor right into the middle of the action, you'll invariably spook the fish.

Hold the boat in position with your trolling motor and make long casts. If you stop the boat on the upwind side of the school, you can use the wind to your advantage for extra casting distance.

When the school breaks up or moves, try vertically jigging for a minute or two to catch any fish near the bottom, but be on the lookout for another flock of birds.

Fish along a treeline to catch temperate bass in open water. The fish use the trees as an edge against which they can trap schools of baitfish.

Use a pair of pliers to flatten the barb of your jig hook; this way, when the bite is on, you can remove the hook in a hurry and save valuable fishing time.

Make a tandem jig set-up by tying a pair of 10-pound-test droppers to a 3-way swivel. With this rig, you'll often catch two fish at a time.

Tip your jig with a strip of belly meat (where legal) from a fish you've already caught. The belly meat not only adds scent, it slows the sink rate, giving the fish more time to strike.

Use a casting bobber to provide the weight necessary to make long casts with a small jig. This way, you can match the size of small baitfish without sacrificing casting distance.

Unusual Opportunities

Although the vast majority of temperate bass are taken by anglers fishing on the spawning grounds or jump-fishing in open water, there are several other good opportunities for fast action—if you know what to look for.

Here are some unusual situations that can provide excellent fishing if you're in the right place at the right time. You may not find the right circumstances on the waters you fish, but you should know about them so you can get in on the action should the opportunity present itself.

In clear lakes, temperate bass often feed heavily at night. Look for them around lighted docks in marinas or use a lantern or crappie light (p. 55) to attract them. Fish with a plain minnow or jig and minnow in the lighted area.

Ice fishermen on northern lakes occasionally find big schools of white bass, usually in the same areas where they found them in late summer and fall. You can catch the fish on small jigging lures, particularly swimming minnows.

In deep reservoirs, large schools of white bass concentrate in deep holes (50 to 80 feet) in the main river channel and in creek channels. Locate these schools with your depth finder and vertically jig with a ½- to 1-ounce jigging spoon.

In winter, warmwater discharges from power plants on big rivers attract huge concentrations of shad which, in turn, draw large numbers of temperate bass. Anglers pitching jigs right into the heated water often catch fish on nearly every cast.

ICE-FISHING FOR PANFISH

*I*ce-fishing can produce even more panfish than open-water fishing—if you know how to find the fish and coax them to bite.

How To Catch Panfish

Ice-Fishing for Panfish

Not too many years ago, most winter panfish anglers simply punched a hole in the ice, lowered a baited hook or teardrop attached to a float and waited patiently for something to pull it under.

While there may be times when that method is still effective, most modern, successful panfishermen use a more active approach: Instead of waiting for the fish to come to them, they go to the fish.

The active approach has been made possible not only by the introduction of better, more portable fishing equipment and better means of traveling on ice, but also by the angler's improved under-standing of their quarry's locational patterns.

In years past, for example, ice fishermen always made an effort to get out on "first ice," because that's when the fish bit best. The hot bite would last a week or two and then many anglers would give up because fishing was just too tough.

While that "early bird" philosophy is still shared by many panfishermen, more and more anglers are now likely to follow the fish into deeper water as the winter progresses. They use ultra-sensitive electronics to locate panfish that may be far from any significant cover or struc-ture and often record catches that are just as good—or better—than those seen in early season.

Anglers who are willing to explore new water have another big advantage over those that stay put. Because they're getting away from the crowd, they're fishing for panfish that are virtually untouched, rather than those that have seen every possible lure or bait dangled in their face. And with no other commotion from other anglers, their augers and their vehicles, the fish are much more likely to be in a cooperative mood.

The secret to successful panfishing is getting away from the crowd.

Improved electronics make it possible for anglers to see the fish (red line) and their lure (green line) and to experiment with different presentations until they find the action that the fish want.

ICE-FISHING EQUIPMENT

In modern ice-fishing, the key word is mobility. No matter if you're fishing for panfish or pike, you must be willing and able to change locations quickly in order to stay with the fish.

This mobility is greatly facilitated by the use of modern electronics. Now you can find a productive spot during the open-water season, enter the waypoint in your GPS and then return unerringly to the same spot once the ice forms.

Once you get there, you can use a lightweight, supersharp ice auger to drill enough holes that you can hop around with a sensitive flasher until you find the fish. The flasher not only shows you where the fish are, it helps you refine your presentation in order to entice them to bite.

If the weather is nice, many anglers opt to fish outside, relying on a down or Thinsulate parka and bibs, boots with space-age insulation and mittens with chemical handwarmers inside to keep warm. This way, they can move about with ease.

In colder weather or when they want to sight-fish, most fishermen prefer a portable, lightweight shelter that can easily be pulled across the ice, carried in the back of a pickup or strapped to the cargo carrier of a snowmobile. Some shelters can be set up and pulled around so easily that it's almost as convenient as fishing outside.

If you're using a fish house big enough for the entire family, relocating is an all-day project, so you're not likely to do it very often. With a big, fancy shack, you can spend the afternoon watching the football game on TV and enjoying a few brews, but don't expect to catch many fish.

Here are some guidelines on selecting the ice-fishing equipment you need along with some suggestions on how to use it.

Selecting a Flasher

A color flasher (left) and a liquid-crystal flasher (right) are both excellent choices. A color flasher shows the fish and the lure in different colors, but the dial is difficult to see in direct sunlight, so you must use some type of hood. A liquid-crystal flasher is easy to see in bright sun and has a backlit screen for night-fishing.

Tips for Using Flashers

Make a hood for a Vexilar color flasher from a 1-pound coffee can. For best visibility, paint the can black.

Outfit a color flasher with a night-light so you can read the dial after dark. Use a 12-volt light that can be wired to the unit's battery.

Use a flasher with a self-leveling transducer. This way, you can pick up the entire unit and set it in another hole without taking time to readjust the transducer.

Other Ice-Fishing Electronics

A handheld GPS not only gets you to spots that would otherwise be nearly impossible to find, it helps you get back to the landing when a snowstorm or white-out obscures visibility.

A flashlight-type sounder makes scouting structure quick and easy. Just squirt a little water on the ice, place the face of the sounder in the water and sound through the ice.

An underwater video camera is ideal for ice-fishing because you can lower it down a hole adjacent to the one in which you're fishing and watch the action just as if you were watching TV. You not only know when there's fish around, you know what kind they are and what size they are. And by observing how they react to your lure, you can adjust your presentation accordingly.

A heavy, well-sharpened ice chisel is a must for early season ice fishing. You can use it for testing ice thickness and for chopping holes in ice less than 6 inches thick.

A supersharp hand auger is ideal when you want to travel extra-light. The 5- or 6-inch sizes normally used for panfishing weigh less than 7 pounds, yet they can easily cut through a foot of ice in 10 seconds.

Remove excess ice from your hole using a sturdy metal, not plastic, ice scoop. When it freezes up, you can tap it on the ice without breaking it, and you can use it to break away new ice that forms in your hole.

Use a lightweight, supersharp gas auger when you want to cut a lot of holes in mid- to late season, when the ice may be up to 3 feet thick. Most panfish anglers prefer 6- or 7-inch models that weigh less than 25 pounds.

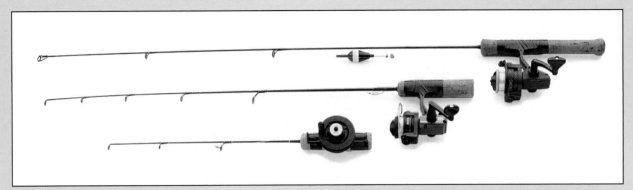

A good panfish rod should be moderately stiff with a tip that will flex enough to signal a subtle panfish bite. For best sensitivity, most anglers use graphite or graphite composite rods. For sight-fishing, you want to be close to the hole, so a 16- to 19-inch rod (bottom) works best. For fishing inside a portable shack with a low roof, use a 24- to 28-inch rod (middle); anything longer will bump the roof when you set the hook. For fishing outside or in a shack with a high roof, use a 30- to 36-inch rod (top); it will give you a better jigging action and a stronger hookset.

Your rod should have lightweight, single-foot guides large enough so they won't freeze shut every few minutes. With large guides, you can easily flick the ice out with your fingers.

Select a light spinning reel with a wide spool to minimize line kinking, and a smooth front drag. Even if the rod has attachment rings, secure the reel with electrical tape so it can't slip.

Use light, extra-limp mono when panfishing through the ice. With tough mono, a lightweight panfish lure can't straighten out the kinks, so bites are difficult to detect.

To detect subtle panfish strikes, use a stiffer rod rigged with a spring bobber. Thread your line through the eye of the spring and down through the rod tip as shown. When you see any unusual movement of the spring, set the hook.

Selecting an Ice Shelter

Fold-up shelters (left) with sides made of canvas or synthetic fabrics set up quite easily and can accommodate two or three anglers. But most models require a good-sized stove with an external propane bottle and not as easy to move as a flip-up shelter (below).

Flip-up shelters come in 1-man (above) and 2-man models. They set up in a few seconds, can be heated with a small, self-contained propane stove (below) and, because they double as a sled, allow excellent mobility.

Ice-Shelter Accessories

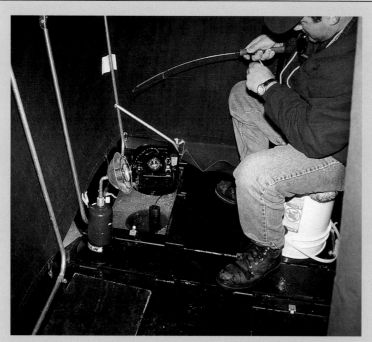

A small, self-starting heater with an attached 1-pound propane bottle is ideal for heating a 1-man shelter. A bottle will last most of the day and the reflector allows you to direct the heat.

Use a battery-powered lantern when fishing in a small shelter. Some models can be powered from your depth finder battery. The fumes produced by a gas lantern can be irritating in a small enclosure.

Customizing Your Portable Ice Shelter

To add a non-skid surface and make clean-up much easier, cut a piece of ¼-inch plywood to fit the floor and staple on some indoor-outdoor carpeting. Do not attach the plywood permanently.

Bolt a fold-up seat to the plywood bench seat to provide more back support. Swivel seats are not really necessary and add unneeded weight.

Drill a hole in the seat of your shelter and attach a spring-coil rod holder, which will help you detect subtle bites (p. 155).

Make a storage tray by bolting a 20-inch length of plastic rain gutter (with end caps) to the side of the plastic base.

Other Ice-Fishing Accessories

As a safety precaution, carry a set of interlocking ice picks in your pocket. Should you fall through, the picks will help you grip the ice and crawl out.

For better traction on glare ice, wear specially designed ice-fishing cleats that fit over your insulated boots.

When fishing outside, carry all your ice-fishing gear in a sturdy molded-plastic sled. Some anglers pull their sled behind a snowmobile or 4-wheeler.

How To Catch Panfish

ICE FISHING FOR SUNFISH

When your rod doubles over as a big bluegill starts making laps around your ice hole, you'll understand why bull 'gills are the favorite of so many ice anglers. It's also possible to catch pumpkinseeds, redears and other kinds of sunfish through the ice, but bluegills are the mainstay.

When & Where

'Gills are easy to find in early winter. Look for them in shallow, weedy bays, on weed flats, in backwaters and in other spots where you would expect to find them in early spring. Spots that still have some green weeds are likely to hold more fish than those that have only brown, decaying weeds.

The fish remain in these shallow, weedy areas for a few weeks, but they soon begin moving to deeper water. By midwinter, you'll find most of them off the edges of weed flats, especially around inside turns on the breakline. Some of the fish move into deep holes and may suspend well off the bottom. But their tendency to suspend is not quite as strong as that of crappies. The action usually slows in midwinter as the oxygen level in the depths gradually declines.

When the spring thaw begins and meltwater starts to replenish oxygen levels, bluegills move back to the shallow bays. The higher oxygen level also activates the fish, so late-season ice anglers enjoy some of the year's fastest action.

Tips for Finding Wintertime Sunfish

Look for sunfish along the outside edge of weedbeds in early winter. You can easily locate some types of emergent weeds, such as bulrushes, by looking for the tips frozen into the ice.

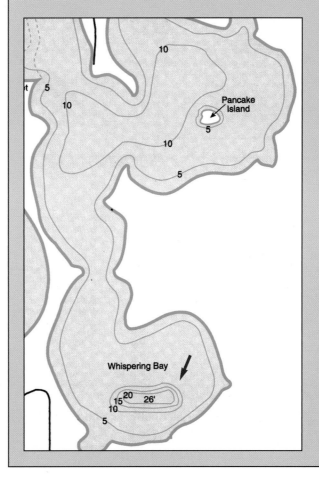

In midwinter, look for sunfish in deep holes (arrow), especially those in a shallow portion of the lake. You can easily pinpoint these spots by referring to a lake map.

Techniques for Winter Sunfish

You can catch sunfish simply by dangling your bait beneath a float, but you'll catch a lot more by jigging. A moving bait will almost always attract more fish and, by using an ultrasensitive graphite jigging rod, you'll be able to detect bites that would go unnoticed with a float.

But there's another even more important reason for jigging: It enables you to move from hole to hole without constantly readjusting your float to match the water depth. As a result, you'll find yourself moving about and covering more water than you otherwise would.

Good electronics are a must in ice fishing for sunfish. Your flasher should be sensitive enough to pick up a tiny jig in 30 feet of water. Then, when the fish are finicky, you can put the bait right in their face and twitch it, jiggle it or slowly lift it to tease them into biting.

In selecting sunfish jigs, the main consideration is water depth. You can use most any jig in water less than 10 feet deep. But in deeper water, you'll need a jig that weighs at least ¹⁄₆₄ ounce, preferably one with a fat lead body. Thin, spoon-type jigs take too long to get down, and they aren't heavy enough to take the coil out of your line. The coils absorb the force of a bite, so you may not even notice when a fish takes your jig. To minimize the coiling problem and line visibility, use limp monofilament of no more than 4-pound test.

Sunfish jigs are usually tipped with some type of grub worm. Waxworms and Eurolarvae are the most popular, but you can also use spikes, mousies, mealworms and goldenrod grubs.

Popular Tipping Baits for Winter Sunfish

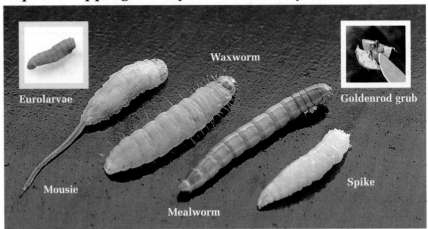

Eurolarvae, Waxworm, Mousie, Mealworm, Goldenrod grub, Spike

Popular Jigging Lures for Sunfish

Fat Boy, Genz Worm, Rat Finkee, Fire-Eye Minnow, Rocker, Purist, Demon, Pounder, Glow Ant, Hackled Ant, Marmooska Jig, Daphnia, Banshee, Moon Glow

Jigging for Sunfish

If your jig has an attachment eye on the back, slide your knot to the top of the eye so the jig rides in a horizontal position (left). If the knot slips to the front of the eye (middle), the jig will ride vertically and will not look natural. Some jigs, such as "teardrops" (right), have the attachment eye at the front; tie them on so they ride vertically.

Hook a large grub, such as a waxworm (left) or mealworm, by threading it on headfirst and then bringing the hook out the side about ¼ inch down so the bait hangs straight on the hook. Smaller grubs, such as Eurolarvae (right) and spikes, are usually hooked through the head end, sometimes two or three at a time.

Lower the jig into the water while watching your flasher. If you see fish, keep your jig just above them; sunfish are more likely to come up for a jig than go down for it.

After lowering the jig to the desired depth, jig it there for (a) several seconds, then pause for a few seconds. After the pause, raise the lure a few inches and repeat the jig-pause-raise sequence (b and c). Work your bait with a gentle jigging motion, varying the action while watching your flasher to see how the fish respond. When you see a fish move rapidly toward your bait, get ready for a bite.

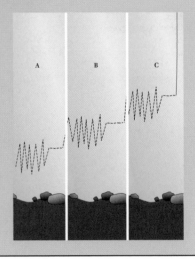

Tips for Catching Sunfish

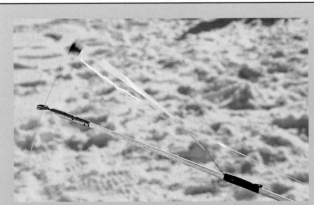

Watch your spring bobber closely while jigging in a slow, methodical fashion. The spring should move in harmony with the rod tip; if it doesn't, set the hook.

Use a trigger-operated spin-cast reel. The closed face prevents build-up of snow and ice on your spool.

ICE-FISHING FOR CRAPPIES

Pulling a "slab" crappie through a hole in the ice is a thrill for any angler. But the nomadic habits of these fish make it difficult to catch them consistently any time of the year, let alone in winter when ice cover limits your mobility. This explains why successful ice anglers spend so much time scouting.

Where & When

Crappie fishing is easiest in early season. The fish will most likely be in shallow, weedy bays or on weed flats—the same areas where you're likely to find sunfish. In fact, it's not uncommon for early-season ice anglers to catch a mixed bag of crappies and sunfish.

But within two or three weeks, the fish begin moving into deeper water where they're a lot tougher to find. There will be times when they'll concentrate around structure such as a hump or an irregularity on the break-line, but they're more likely to suspend in a deep hole far from any kind of structure.

If you regularly fish a particular body of water, you probably know where these crappie holes are; the fish tend to use the same ones year after year. Otherwise, get a good hydrographic map and look for the deepest holes, particularly those surrounded by relatively shallow water.

If the ice is not too slushy or milky, you may be able to find the fish without drilling holes. With a sensitive flasher and a squirt bottle, you can sound right through the ice to locate the fish (above right).

Winter crappies tend to bite best early or late in the day and, in very clear lakes, they may not start biting until well after dark.

How to Find Wintertime Crappies

Scout for crappies by finding a deep hole and then walking around with a flasher and squirt bottle. Spray a little water on the ice, hold your transducer in the puddle and watch the dial. Because crappies usually suspend well off the bottom, they're easy to spot.

Once you find some fish, drill lots of holes in the surrounding area. This way, you can easily move about to stay with the fish when they move.

Techniques for Winter Crappies

Dangling a lively minnow beneath a small float has long been the favorite technique of most wintertime crappie fishermen. The method works well anytime you have the fish pinpointed and is particularly effective in very clear lakes where crappies sometimes refuse anything but real food.

But winter crappies seldom stay put for long. So rather than wait them out with a minnow rig, more and more anglers are using jigging techniques to greatly increase their mobility.

Because crappies eat so many small fish, it's easy to understand why swimming minnows, such as Normark's Jigging Rapala (size 2 or 3), are the most popular type of jigging lure. These heavy lead-bodied baits not only sink quickly to get you into deepwater crappie haunts, the plastic tail fin makes them dart to the side when you jig. In 30 feet of water, for example, the bait glides 4 to 5 feet on each jigging stroke, enabling you to cover an 8- to 10-foot circle. Swimming minnows have a realistic look, so you don't have to tip

Float-Fishing for Crappies

Basic Rig:

Float—Peg-on float.

Hook—Size 4 short-shank bait hook.

Weight—Enough split shot to balance your float.

Bait—1½-inch fathead or shiner minnow hooked through the back.

If you see fish on your depth finder, attach a clip-on weight (inset) and lower it until it is just above the fish. Then peg your float in place, pull up your line, remove the weight, add a minnow and lower it back down. If you don't see fish, keep changing depths until you start getting bites.

When your float goes down, grab the rod and set the hook. You can set much more easily with a rod than you could by jerking on the line. After the fish is hooked, pull in the line hand over hand, coiling it neatly on the ice to avoid tangling.

them with live bait. But tipping them with a minnow
head is an option.

You can also jig for crappies with the same small jig-
grub combos used for sunfish,
but these baits are hard to use
in deep water because it takes
so long for them to sink.

A medium-power graphite
jigging rod and a small spinning reel spooled with 4- to
6-pound mono works well for
both float-fishing and jigging.

Popular Jigging Lures for Winter Crappies

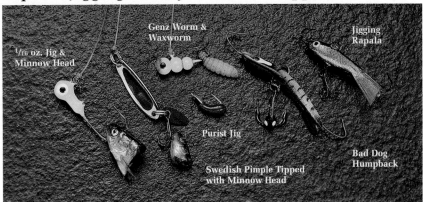

How to Fish a Swimming Minnow

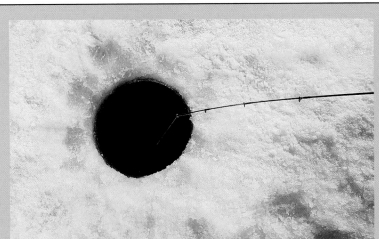

Give the lure a sharp upward twitch, then return the rod to
the starting position and hold the tip still. The line will
move off to one side (shown) and then slowly settle back to
the middle. Wait until the line stops moving before you jig
again; practically all strikes come on the pause. If you feel a
light tap, a nudge or anything out of the ordinary, set the
hook.

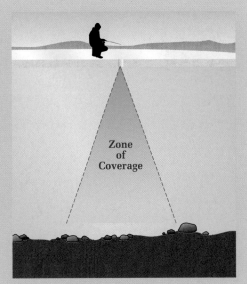

A swimming minnow covers a large
area around the hole. The diameter of
the coverage zone increases as the
water gets deeper.

Tips for Catching Crappies

Use a sponge-float in cold
weather. When the float
ices up, just squeeze it and
the ice crumbles away.

Use a slip-float
at above-
freezing tem-
peratures. This
way, you can
reel your line
through the
float rather
than pulling it
in by hand.

Tip a swimming minnow by
pushing one prong of the
bottom treble hook through
the lips of a minnow head.

ICE-FISHING FOR PERCH

If you've ever fried up a batch of yellow perch fillets, you'll understand why there's been such an explosion of interest in ice-fishing for these scrappy panfish.

Another reason for their increasing popularity: Perch abound in practically all northern lakes that have decent walleye populations. The challenge is finding waters that have good-sized perch.

When & Where

You can find small to medium-sized perch in practically any walleye lake. But few lakes have good numbers of "jumbo" perch (those weighing 12 ounces or more) and lakes with super-jumbos (1½-plus pounders) are a real rarity.

Your odds of finding big perch are greatest in large midwestern walleye lakes, primarily those with a surface area of more than 20,000 acres.

You may also find big perch in a few smaller "freeze-out" lakes, but populations in these waters are highly variable, depending on when the last freeze-out occurred. The biggest perch are usually found in highly fertile lakes that abound with *gammarus*, tiny freshwater shrimp that make perfect perch food.

If you know where to find walleyes in a particular lake, you should have no trouble finding perch. Both use the

To locate perch spread over a large flat, scatter some tip-ups baited with minnows. When you find some fish, try jigging in the same area.

If you've been catching perch on a drop-off but they stop biting, try drilling some holes far off the structure where the bottom flattens out. Perch may often move several hundred yards from the structure in midday and then return to the structure toward evening.

same type of structure, although perch often move away from the structure and can be found over a flat, muddy bottom, especially in midday.

Big perch are known for their finicky feeding habits. Sometimes they turn on at dusk and dawn; other times, in midday. The pattern can change daily and seems to bear little relationship to the weather.

Perch fishing is usually good in early and late winter, but the best bite of all is in very late winter, when the ice starts to honeycomb.

Techniques for Winter Perch

You could easily catch the biggest yellow perch with a light jigging rod and 2- to 4-pound test line, but many anglers prefer heavier tackle in case they hook a nice walleye—which is a distinct possibility in most good perch waters. A sensitive, medium-power graphite rod and a small spinning reel spooled with 6-pound mono is a good choice where the walleye option exists.

Although many wintertime perch are caught by bobber fishing with a plain minnow, jigging will almost always produce more fish. Of course, jigging makes you a lot more mobile, but that's not the only reason. The jigging action will often tease the fish into biting.

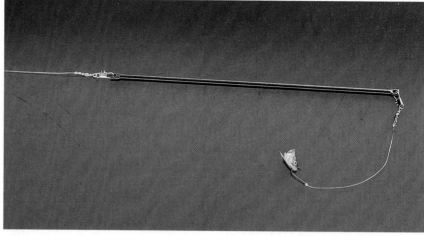

Draw the attention of perch with a hanger rig, which is an 8- to 12-inch metal rod with a short dropper and a hook, or just a hook, at the end. Bait up with a minnow head, perch eye or grub and bounce the rig on the bottom to stir up silt.

Winter perch fishermen use surprisingly large jigging lures (below), often the same ones used by walleye anglers in the same area. Small lures, such as a teardrop tipped with waxworms, will also catch plenty of perch, but the fish usually run on the small side.

Whatever lure you use, be sure to periodically drop it to the bottom to kick up mud. Perch commonly root mayfly wigglers and other larval insects out of the muck, so they're attracted by the cloud of silt. Their insect-eating habits also explain why a hanger rig (above) is so effective.

Catching perch is easy when the bite is on, but the best perch fishermen have a bag of tricks that put fish on the ice even when the bite is slow (opposite).

There's no doubt that wintertime perch fishing can be tough: It's an open-water proposition, and a school can be here one minute and gone the next. You have to be mobile, you have to keep trying different things, and you must keep your bait moving. The rewards for all the work —some fast action followed by superb eating—are well worth the effort.

Popular Lures & Baits for Winter Perch

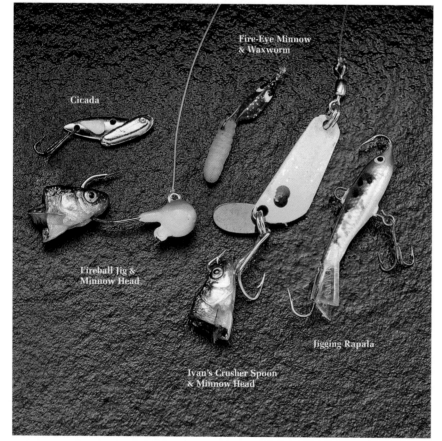

Cicada

Fire-Eye Minnow & Waxworm

Fireball Jig & Minnow Head

Ivan's Crusher Spoon & Minnow Head

Jigging Rapala

Remove the hook from a jigging spoon and replace it with a size 6 single hook on a 4-inch, 6-pound-test mono dropper. Bait the hook with a minnow head, a perch eye, a mayfly wiggler or a couple of waxworms. Lower the rig to within 6 inches of the bottom, lift it a foot or so, and let it flutter back down.

If nothing bites after jigging with your dropper rig for awhile, set your rod in a rod holder. Adjust the depth so the hook of your dropper rig is just above the bottom, then sit back and watch the rod tip. If it wiggles even the slightest bit, set the hook.

If your depth finder shows perch hanging near your bait but not biting, try teasing them up. Lift the bait slowly, jigging it a little along the way and then pausing to give the fish a chance to bite. Perch may follow the bait for 10 or even 20 feet and then grab it at the last minute so it doesn't get away.

When fishing is extra-tough, try a mayfly wiggler threaded headfirst onto a size 10 Aberdeen hook, preferably on a dropper rig. Although wigglers are very delicate and difficult to keep on the hook, they'll produce perch when nothing else will.

INDEX